Isabella Andreini

LA MIRTILLA: A PASTORAL

Medieval and Renaissance Texts and Studies

Volume 242

GELOSA + ISABELLA ANDREINI COMICA

HOC. HISTRICÆ. ELOQVENTIÆ. CAPVT.
LECTOR. ADMIRARIS?
BENÈ. HABET.
QVID. SI. AVDITOR. SIES?

Pola.

Raphael Sadeler scalpsit. 1602.

Portrait of Isabella Andreini by Raphail Sadeler.
Reproduced by permission of The Newberry Library.

Isabella Andreini

LA MIRTILLA: A PASTORAL

Translated with an Introduction and Notes

by

JULIE D. CAMPBELL

Arizona Center for Medieval and Renaissance Studies
Tempe, Arizona
2002

Library of Congress Cataloging-in-Publication Data

Andreini, Isabella, 1562–1604.
   [Mirtilla. English]
   La Mirtilla : a pastoral / Isabella Andreini ; translated with an introduction and
notes by Julie D. Campbell.
      p. cm. — (Medieval and Renaissance texts and studies ; v. 242)
   Includes bibliographical references.
   ISBN 0-86698-284-1 (alk. paper)
   I. Campbell, Julie D., 1965– II. Title. III. Medieval & Renaissance Texs &
Studies (Series) ; 242.

PQ4562.A72 M5713 2002
852'.5—dc21
                                              2002018436

∞
This book is made to last.
It is set in Garamond Antiqua typeface,
smythe-sewn and printed on acid-free paper
to library specifications.

Printed in the United States of America

For Don and Sharon Campbell
and
Niny Stelly

CONTENTS

ACKNOWLEDGMENTS

My work on this translation has been generously supported by a Texas A&M Women's Studies Fellowship, which funded research at the Newberry Library, and a Texas A&M Association of Former Students/Office of Graduate Studies Award, which enabled me to research Andreini's texts at the Biblioteca Marciana in Venice. Further research was supported in part by an NEH Summer Stipend and an Eastern Illinois University Summer Research Award. I owe a great deal of thanks to Giovanna Ulrici, Riccardo Rigon, and Paolo D'Odorico who maintained contact with the helpful staff at the Biblioteca Marciana for me after my initial visit there and facilitated my orders for microfilm. I also thank Professor Federica Ambrosini of the Dipartimento di Storia at the Università degli Studi di Padova for her willingness to recommend useful Italian texts on Andreini. I am grateful to the staff of the Sterling Evans Library at Texas A&M, especially Wendi Arant Kaspar and John P. Fullerton, for their assistance with a variety of searches and quests for microfilm. I am, as always, indebted to my Italian tutor and mentor, Mrs. Maria Amalia Stelly, for her invaluable help and encouragement. I also owe a great deal to Dr. Leslie S. B. MacCoull and the anonymous readers for MRTS for their corrections and editorial advice, as well as for their enthusiastic support of this project. For his advice on bibliographic matters, I thank James Harner, and for his advice on research in Italian libraries and archives, I thank Craig Kallendorf. For her early encouragement of my interest in Andreini, I am grateful to Anne MacNeil, and for her long-standing support of my interest in early modern women's literary history, I thank Margaret Ezell. Finally, special thanks go to Joan Burton at Trinity University in San Antonio, Texas, and to Mardell O'Brien and Bruce Swann of the Classics Library at the University of Illinois for their expert help in tracking the "famous" plane-tree.

INTRODUCTION

The developments of the *commedia dell'arte* and the *commedia erudita* have been well documented by scholars of Italian Renaissance drama and literature. One figure whose work flourished during the height of both these styles' popularity is Isabella Andreini (1562–1604), an actress, poet, playwright, and member of the prestigious academy, the Intenti of Pavia. While her fame as one of the greatest *innamorate* in the history of Italian comedy has been frequently noted, as has her co-direction with her husband Francesco Andreini of the celebrated company, the Gelosi,[1] her texts have yet to be widely considered with regard to their place in women's literary history and in the canon of Renaissance literature. Increasing interest in Renaissance women writers in general, and the rise of new Andreini scholarship by such writers as Anne MacNeil, Louise George Clubb, and Maria Luisa Doglio in particular,[2] suggest that the time is right for English translations of Andreini's literary endeavors.[3] A popular success, *La Mir-*

---

[1] K. M. Lea notes that "with the exception of an appearance among the Confidenti in Genova [in] 1589 and among the Uniti in 1601, Isabella was the 'prima donna' of the Gelosi" (*Italian Popular Comedy*, 2 vols. [New York: Russell and Russell, 1962], 499). For an overview of the major companies of this period, including the Gelosi, see Kenneth and Laura Richards, *The Commedia dell'Arte: A Documentary History* (Oxford: Basil Blackwell-Shakespeare Head Press, 1990), 55–69.

[2] For more references to scholarship on Andreini and *La Mirtilla*, see the *Nota bibliografica* in Maria Luisa Doglio's introduction to Isabella Andreini, *La Mirtilla* (Lucca: Fazzi, 1995), 20; Laura Anna Stortoni and Mary Prentice Lillie, *Women Poets of the Italian Renaissance* (New York: Italica, 1997), 224–25; and Anne Elizabeth MacNeil, "Music and the Life and Work of Isabella Andreini: Humanistic Attitudes toward Music, Poetry, and Theater During the Late Sixteenth and Early Seventeenth Centuries" (Ph.D. diss., University of Chicago, 1994), 462–86. Further new commentary on the Andreini will be available in MacNeil's book on the Andreini family and music in the *commedia dell'arte*, which is slated for publication by Oxford University Press in 2002.

[3] Stortoni and Lillie have included translated excerpts from Andreini's poetry, prose, and drama in their anthology *Women Poets of the Italian Renaissance*, but no complete English translation of her comic masterpiece *La Mirtilla* has previously been available. In addition to *La Mirtilla*, Andreini wrote her *Rime* (1601), around five hundred lyric poems and a few pastoral eclogues; her *contrasti scenici,* the dialogues which she wrote and co-wrote with Francesco, published in *Fragmenti di alcune scritture della Signora Isabella Andreini*

tilla was published just before Battista Guarini's *Il pastor fido* (1590), and the 1588 edition sold out quickly. Ultimately, it was printed nine times by 1616 in a variety of editions and reprints in several cities in Italy, as well as Paris.

A highly accomplished woman, Andreini embodied both humanist and Christian ideals for early modern women, attributes considered unusual in an actress. She was born Isabella Canali in Padua, of obscure family origins, a fact which has led scholars to suggest that she was trained to become a courtesan. Rosalind Kerr notes that "her education in the fine arts supports the evidence that she began her training as an 'honest courtesan'" ("The Actress as Androgyne," 64). Whether or not she was meant to be a courtesan, the facts remain that Isabella married Francesco de'Cerrachi Andreini of Pistoia at age sixteen and that her public reputation for virtue increased throughout her life. Rinaldina Russell notes that although "scandal, travel, and the disturbances actresses incited encouraged society to view them as little better than courtesans ...," the "erudite Isabella Canali Andreini, distinguished poet and faithful wife of the comic actor Francesco Andreini, enhanced the respectability of her profession" (*Feminist Encyclopedia*, 6). A devoted wife and the mother of seven children, she was widely praised for her virtue and piety. One of her contemporaries eulogized her as a "Comica saggia, gratiosa, e bella / Dotata di virtù superbe, e rare ..." [Comedienne (or actress) wise, gracious, and beautiful / endowed with virtues superb and rare ...].[4] This image endured, prompting nineteenth-century critic Defendente Sacchi to compare her to Vittoria Colonna.[5] Ultimately, her literary and dramatic talents and her reputation as a virtuous and learned woman shaped her lasting public image.[6]

Andreini also moved gracefully between the worlds of the stage and academic circles.[7] With the Gelosi she performed throughout Italy and

---

... (1620); and her *Lettere* (1602), numerous philosophical arguments on a wide variety of topics. For a list of Andreini's publications, see MacNeil, "Life and Work," 465.

[4] The description is from the poem by Iacom'antonio Tassoni, Academico Inquieto, in the introductory material to the 1605 edition of *La Mirtilla*, published in Milan.

[5] Andreini died during a miscarriage of her eighth child at age forty-two in Lyons, France. Her fame was such that she was allowed a state funeral by the French royal family. Afterwards, medallions with her image on them were cast and inscribed with the words "Eterna Fama" or Eternal Fame (MacNeil, "Life and Work," 20; Doglio, introduction to *La Mirtilla*, 19). On Sacchi's commentary, see MacNeil, "Life and Work," 21–22.

[6] Upon her death, Francesco retired to Mantua where he wrote of his grief over her death and published her poetry and letters along with his own compositions for theater (Louise George Clubb, *Italian Drama in Shakespeare's Time* [New Haven: Yale University Press, 1989], 260).

[7] In *Storia delle Accademie d'Italia*, Michele Maylender notes the membership of the "celebrated comic Gelosa Isabella Andreini" in his entry on the Intenti of Pavia, discussing her connections with the academy (vol. 3, 319–23). In addition to being a member of the

France, enjoying the patronage of the Este, Gonzaga, and Medici families, as well as the French royals. As far as literary alliances were concerned, Andreini was a friend of Torquato Tasso, whose play *Aminta* (1573) she imitates in *La Mirtilla*. Her prowess at lyric poetry is often illustrated by the story that she participated in a poetry contest with Tasso in Rome, taking second place to his first. Some, including Angelo Solerti, have argued that such a contest never took place.[8] Whether or not the story is true, it is clear that Tasso was an important influence on Andreini. In his 1984 article "Bella d'Asia: Torquato Tasso, gli attori e l'immortalità," Ferdinando Taviani examines the relationship between Tasso and the Andreini family, commenting especially on his friendship with Isabella. He explores the worlds of letters and theatre that brought Tasso and Isabella together, noting that through the latter Isabella was exposed to "la fama" and "la diffamazione" [the fame and the defamation] of the acting milieu, and he discusses how she achieved her "virtuosa" status ("Bella d'Asia," 4–5). He also comments on her literary career, arguing that her rapport with Tasso was instrumental in aiding her rise from the ranks of common actors (45).

While her literary works were acclaimed by such contemporaries as Jacopo Castelvetro, Gabriello Chiabrera, Ridolfo Campeggi, and Ercole Tasso, her status as an Intenta placed her in contact with other supporters who would serve as patrons, including Carlo Emmanuele II, the duke of Savoy, and Ranuccio Farnese, the duke of Parma.[9] Above all, Andreini's writing testifies to her rich humanist education, which she cultivated throughout her life. One especially significant example is her correspondence with Ericius Puteanus,[10] a fellow Intento and Milanese professor of classical languages. MacNeil notes that this exchange is particularly revealing because it documents Andreini's discussion of her efforts to use "classical allusions, scholarly allegories, and *double entendres*" in her works, and it proves that she "read Latin texts of considerable difficulty."[11] Evidence

---

Intenti, she was connected with other academies in Italy, including the Accademia Filarmonica of Verona and the Accademia Olimpica of Vicenza (MacNeil, "Life and Work," 49).

[8] See MacNeil on Solerti ("Life and Work," 19–20).

[9] For more on the poetry contest and the records of Andreini's activities with the Intenti and other academies, see MacNeil, "Life and Work," 9, 48–52 and Clubb, *Italian Drama*, 260. For an overview of Andreini's travels with the Gelosi and engagements performed for their patrons, see MacNeil, "Life and Work," 36–41 and Clubb, *Italian Drama*, 262–66.

[10] Ericius Puteanus was also known as Ericio Puteano, Henri de Put, Henri Pute, Henri Dupuis, and Hendrick van der Putte (MacNeil, "Life and Work," 43).

[11] MacNeil has documented Andreini's correspondence with Puteanus ("Life and Work," 45–48) and transcribed their extant letters (403–34). For more information on early modern female Latinists, see Jane Stevenson, "Women and Classical Education in the Early Modern Period" in *Pedagogy and Power: Rhetorics of Classical Learning*, ed. Yun Lee Too and Niall Livingstone, Ideas in Context 50 (Cambridge: Cambridge University Press, 1998),

of her diverse education and her command of classical sources, combined with her intimate understanding of drama, resonates throughout her play.

La Mirtilla is permeated with references to classical sources that Andreini recycles at will to support and garnish her plot. Many of these references are identified in footnotes throughout the text; however, a brief consideration of her adaptations here illustrates Andreini's manipulation of these images and ideas. In 2.1.938, Ardelia retorts, "Più tosto tornerà l'antico caos / che in me s'annidi mai pensier d'amore" [Sooner the ancient chaos will return / than in me will ever be harbored thought of love!], echoing the line from Ovid's *Metamorphoses* (2.299) in which Earth prays to be saved from Phaeton's fire, fearing that all will be hurled "[i]nto the ancient chaos."[12] Ardelia's use of the expression illustrates the extreme, even hubristic, nature of her refusal to consider love, which makes her seduction by Uranio all the more dramatic. In 3.3.1609 and 5.8.3191–3193, Gorgo praises Bacchus and Ceres, noting in the latter that "di Cerere e di Bacco i frutti amati / ti dono, perché i tuoi cari tesori / senza questi sarian freddi e gelati" [The beloved fruits of Ceres and Bacchus / I give you, for without these / your dear treasures will be cold and frozen]. Here Andreini incorporates a saying from Terence's *Eunuchus*, line 732, "sine Cerere et Libero friget Venus": "without Ceres and Bacchus, Love grows cold," or as John Sargeaunt puts it, "without Ceres and Bacchus Venus is a-chill."[13] Her repetition of this proverb with its emphasis on both the physical and emotional aspects of love illustrates an underlying theme in the play, that of balance and moderation in love.

Moreover, pastoral staples, a number of which may be found in the works of Theocritus and Virgil, inform Andreini's imagery. In Theocritus's *Thyrsis*, for example, the goatherd offers Thyrsis a beautiful cup as an incentive to sing "The Affliction of Daphnis." The goatherd describes the decorations on the carved wooden cup, which include a beautiful woman

---

83–109. Stevenson explores the history of training women in classical languages, especially Latin, and she points out that it is possible "to construct a continuous tradition of women's poetry in Latin from antiquity to the eighteenth century" (94). Stevenson excludes Andreini from her discussion of Italian female Latinists, probably because Andreini wrote primarily in Italian, but her general discussion of the circumstances of Olympia Morata, Cassandra Fedele, Angela and Isotta Nogarola, Laurentia Strozzi and others underscores the privileged position in society that Andreini enjoyed as an actress, wife, mother, and writer/scholar. Stevenson discusses the idea that a "female scholar was expected to be a virgin ... (whose) position was understood by male contemporaries as that of a Sybl or a Muse rather than a co-worker" (101). She notes a select few Italian women who managed to marry and maintain their status as scholars of note, but she emphasizes that such a transition was rare.

[12] Ovid, "The Story of Phaeton" in *Metamorphoses*, trans. Rolfe Humphries (Bloomington: Indiana University Press, 1983), 28–40.

[13] Terence, *The Eunuch* in *Terence*, trans. John Sargeaunt, 2 vols. Vol. 1, The Loeb Classical Library (Cambridge, MA: Harvard University Press, 1939), 232–351.

with two suitors, a fisherman, and a little boy looking over a vineyard, accompanied by two foxes, all beautifully wrought. In exchange for the cup, Thyrsis agrees to sing to for the goatherd (1. 15–63). In 5.1.2655–2684 of *La Mirtilla*, Tirsi beseeches Mirtilla to yield to his proposal and offers her a cup carved from beechwood to help persuade her. On his cup is depicted Diana or "... la luna / in atto di lasciva / e boscareccia ninfa" [... the moon / in the pose / of a lascivious, / sylvan nymph] who consorts with Endimion. An angry Pan who discovers the pair is shown emerging from a nearby wood. Unlike Thyrsis, however, Mirtilla rejects the cup and Tirsi's proposal, at least for the moment. Another potentially influential reference to decorative cups may be seen in Virgil's third eclogue, where carved beech cups serve as suggested currency for a wager between Menalcas and Damœtas, but it is an offer that Damœtas rejects because he already has his own carved cups (lines 35–49).[14] In *Thyrsis*, Theocritus also provides other models for adaptation by Andreini, including the allusion to singing contests between shepherds (lines 24–27) and the goatherd who refers with relish to food and drink (lines 148–50). Theocritus's *Country Singing-Match*, in which Damœtas and Daphnis compete to a draw, also recalls the contest between Mirtilla and Filli, as do the singing contests in *The Harvest-Home* and the *Second* and the *Third Country Singing-Match*.[15] Virgil's third eclogue also contains a reference to a singing contest in line 21; of course, this device may be found throughout pastoral literature. Finally, in 5.2.2724–2729, Andreini's Igilio is reminiscent of Virgil's Gallus from the tenth eclogue. Like Gallus, Igilio carves his love's name on the trees in the woods so that as they grow, so will his love. Poor Gallus dies for unrequited love, but Igilio is saved by the last-minute intervention of his beloved Filli in 5.2.2726. This selection of Andreini's adaptations of classical sources illustrates not only her knowledge of such sources, but also her talent for imbuing them with *commedia dell'arte* dramatic flare. Last-minute rescues of lovers determined to die for love and heroines who participate in singing contests, reject bribes, and swear dangerous oaths that ring with classical overtones prove an entertaining combination, rich in cultural capital.[16]

---

[14] Virgil, *Eclogues*, trans. C. S. Calverley, Bohn's Popular Library (London: G. Bell and Sons, 1913), 186–230.

[15] Theocritus, *Thyrsis* in *The Greek Bucolic Poets*, trans. J. M. Edmonds, The Loeb Classical Library (Cambridge, MA: Harvard University Press, 1960), 9–23. In the same volume, see *Country Singing-Match*, 83–89; *The Harvest Home*, 91–107; *The Second Country Singing-Match*, 109–21; and *The Third Country Singing-Match*, 123–27.

[16] See Pierre Bordieu's evaluation of the weight and worth of cultural capital from "The Forms of Capital" in the *Handbook of Theory and Research for the Sociology of Education*, ed. John G. Richardson (New York: Greenwood Press, 1986), 243–58.

In addition to classical sources, Andreini, like her male contemporaries, closely imitates aspects of Petrarch's *Canzoniere* in many instances in the play. A few examples illustrate her adherence to his style. Like Petrarch, Andreini refers to nymphs' cruel natures by comparing them to wild beasts. In 4.1.1991, she writes that because of their "ferità," the lovers lose their lives. Petrarch makes the same comparison in such poems as number 22, a sestina, in which he writes, "Non credo che pascesse mai per selva / si aspra fera, o di notte o di giorno, / come costei ch'i' piango ..." [I think there never grazed in any wood / so cruel a beast, whether by night or day, / as she for whom I weep ...] and in number 152, a sonnet, in which he writes, "Questa umil fera, un cor di tigre d'orsa / che 'n vista umana o 'n forma d'angel vene" [This kind, wild beast, this tiger's heart or bear's / that comes in human shape or form of angel].[17] Her repeated use of "lumi" or "luci," lights, to describe the eyes of a beloved is a familiar echo from many of Petrarch's poems, including sonnets 198 and 258. Her use of the term "guerra," too, meaning war, in Tirsi's speech (5.6.3033–3034), in which he says, "e ben son lieto e fortunato in terra / poscia che la mia guerra è qui finita" [So, I am truly happy and fortunate on earth / since my war here is finished] echoes Petrarch's use of the word to describe the tumultous effects of love in sonnet 134, "Pace non trovo et non ò da far guerra" [I find no peace, and I am not at war], or in sonnet 96, "Io son de l'aspettar omai si vinto / et de la lunga guerra de'sospiri" [I am so tired now of all this waiting / and of the battle I wage with my sighs]. In 4.2.2361–2364, Coridone describes his beloved Nisa's effect on nature as she walks, noting that wherever she goes, her "bianco piede / nascer fa gigli e rose" [white foot / causes lilies and roses to bloom], which echoes Petrarch's sonnet 165, lines 1–4, in which a force from "'l candido pie'" [the white foot] of his beloved "i fiori apra" [opens the flowers]. In general, Andreini draws heavily upon imagery from the *Canzoniere* to fashion a sun-dappled world of hills and streams, cool, shady caves and woods, and pastures studded with brilliantly colored flowers. Against this backdrop, her characters sing, debate, and find themselves ensnared in all manner of Amore's traps.

In *La Mirtilla* we may see an amalgam of Andreini's cultural interests — poetry, drama, classical mythology, music, literary theory, Platonic philosophy, and popular topics of debate that stem in part from the *questioni d'amore*, the questions about love frequently used as commonplaces to spark discussion in medieval courtly circles and later in Renaissance litera-

---

[17] Translations from Petrarch's *Canzoniere* are by Mark Musa (Bloomington: Indiana University Press, 1996).

ry salons (in Italy, the *ridotti*) and academies.[18] Ultimately, the play is a
sophisticated display of erudition combined with a wicked sense of humor
with regard to the foibles of lovers. In the style of the period, making use
of *imitatio*, Andreini, like Guarini, Samuel Daniel, Lady Mary Wroth, and
many others, imitates, yet adapts, the conceits of Tasso's *Aminta*. In the
process, she creates a pastoral tragicomedy that provides an element long
missing from the traditional canonical studies of this subgenre of drama:
the voice of the Renaissance female dramatist writing in response to the
texts of her male contemporaries.

In the preface to her Italian edition of *La Mirtilla*, published in 1995,
Doglio links Andreini with the line of non-dramatic pastoral writers descending from Virgil, noting also the influences of Ovid, Petrarch, Poli-
ziano, and Sannazaro in her work. Further, Doglio contends that the
speeches of Filli, the role Andreini is said to have reserved for herself,[19]
especially indicate Andreini's place in the line of Italian Renaissance wom-
en poets that includes Veronica Gambara, Gaspara Stampa, and Veronica
Franco ("Introduction," 9–10). Doglio argues that like these poets, Filli
"exprime direttamente il suo tormento" [directly expresses her torment]
and that throughout the play she acts within "un riconosciuto spazio di
autonomia intellettuale" [a recognized space of intellectual autonomy] (9).
These characteristics are especially worthy of note as the play unfolds because it is Filli who participates in Andreini's subversion of the traditional
theatergram,[20] the damsel in distress, and who, along with Mirtilla, values
female friendship over unrequited love (3.4).

Andreini's inclusion of a heroine who is frank, intellectually astute, and
free from many of the obtusely "virtuous" characteristics seen in her foil
Ardelia constitutes a critical moment in the development of the pastoral
tragicomedy and in Renaissance literary characterization in general. When
Andreini's strategies for character development are compared with those
by other writers of the period, interesting similarities and striking dif-
ferences may be observed. Her spunky, self-reflective character Filli brings
to mind Tullia d'Aragona's self-portrayal in her dialogue *Della infinità*

---

[18] Not coincidentally, issues raised in Andreini's *contrasti scenici* also strongly recall the
questioni d'amore. Echoes of her *contrasti* appear in debates throughout the play, as do virtu-
oso displays of *sprezzatura* — the ability to be quick-witted and sharp, as well as to appear
learned, in one's responses, a quality greatly valued in debate exchanges.

[19] See also Taviani, "Bella d'Asia," 8.

[20] Clubb defines theatergrams as the "units, figures, relationships, actions, topoi, and
framing patterns" used throughout Renaissance drama that were gleaned from classic examples and modified with use until they constituted a "combinatory of theatergrams that were
at once streamlined structures for svelte play-making and elements of high specific density,
weighty with significance from previous incarnations" (*Italian Drama*, 6).

di amore (1547) which she wrote in response to Sperone Speroni's *Dialogo di amore* (1542). In Speroni's dialogue, the character Tullia is a stereotypical courtesan, lusty and ruled mainly by her passions, incapable of serious intellectual reason. Tullia's literary rebuttal, however, sharply corrects his vision. In her piece, she characterizes herself as a Renaissance intellectual, interested in mathematics, literature, science, and philosophy, as well as debates over the nature of love. Like the other Renaissance women poets noted above, D'Aragona and Andreini use their literary talents to do their own self-fashioning — and their views on what constitutes the ideal Renaissance woman often diverge considerably from those of their male contemporaries.

Especially in her characterizations of Filli and Ardelia, Andreini provides her audience a singularly humorous glimpse of what the traditionally silent, chaste, and obedient Renaissance beloved might be like, if she were provided a voice and the agency to interact with her admirers, including her pastoral arch-enemy, the satyr.[21] In *Aminta, Il pastor fido*, and other male-authored tragicomedies, such as Shakespeare's *A Midsummer Night's Dream* and Daniel's *The Queen's Arcadia*, heroines are threatened with rape, murder, and loss of reputation until they are rescued by a hero, a judgment by a patriarchal figure, or supernatural intervention. These heroines are remarkable, ultimately, for their lack of agency and their dependency on others to ensure their safety and happiness. In the traditional damsel-in-distress theatergram, for example, in the third act of *Aminta*, Thirsis recounts the story of how Silvia was "Fast fettred by the faire haire to a tree" (3.1.55)[22] by a satyr who stripped her naked and tormented her until Aminta rescued her. With relish, Thirsis describes how even the tree itself aided in the attack:

> For by her feete a branch or two grew out,
> Which (easie bending) both her tender leggs
> Had fastned to the tree. (62–64)

He adds,

---

[21] In "*La castità conquistata*: The Function of the Satyr in Pastoral Drama," Meredith Kennedy Ray explores the comic and violent functions of the satyr in Giovambattista Giraldi Cinzio's *Egle*, Agostino Beccari's *Il sacrificio*, Tasso's *Aminta*, Guarini's *Pastor fido*, and Andreini's *Mirtilla*. She convincingly argues that "the satyr's role as de-stabilizing sexual element can offer a useful key for thinking about the interaction between the Renaissance taste for literary imitation and the elevation of female chastity as a cultural and social ideal" (313).

[22] The translator of the passages from the *Aminta* is Henry Reynolds, whose text (1627) has been edited by Elizabeth Story Donno in *Three Renaissance Pastorals* (Binghamton, NY: Medieval and Renaissance Texts and Studies, 1993), 1–54.

All the defences shee could (poore soule) shee made;
But sure 'twould have but little steeded her,
Had not we come. Aminta with his dart
Flue like a Lyon
Upon the Satyr ... (67–71)

In this play, the "poore soule" Silvia has no recourse but to await rescue
by Aminta, who before saving her takes a moment to

... feast his greedy eyes with her faire limbes,
Which trembling seem'd as tender, white, and soft,
As unprest curds new from the whey divided. (73–75)

Ultimately, Silvia is a victim of both the Satyr's violence and the invasive
gaze of Aminta and his sidekick Thirsis. In spite of Thirsis's assurances
that "shee had no cause to feare; / so modest and respectfull was Aminta"
(116–117), one has the sense that she has been violated anyway, a circum-
stance that Andreini carefully sidesteps in her play.

In keeping with her allegiance to *Aminta*, Andreini has a similar situation occur in Act Three of *La Mirtilla*. Andreini, however, takes liberties
with the traditional theatergram. Like Melidia in Agostino Beccari's *Il sacrificio* (1554), who mistakenly falls into the satyr's trap, but frees herself
by her wits, only to clear the way for the intended victim, Stellinia,[23]
Filli manages to extricate herself from a potential rape. She, however, is
the only nymph caught in the Satyr's trap in this play, and she teaches him
a lesson that promises to put an end to his violent and misogynist ways for
good.[24] At the end of 3.1, after a lengthy soliloquy about how he has
long lusted after Filli, Satiro announces that he will hide behind a bush so
that when she comes by, he may confront her. He swears,

E s'ella al mio voler non sarà presta,
le faró mille oltraggi.
Né sua bellezza voglio che le giovi
né gli alti gridi o 'l domandar mercede. (1285–1288)

[And if she will not surrender to my will, / I will do her a thousand outrages! / Neither her beauty nor her loud cries / or her request for mercy will help her!]

---

[23] Ray traces the development of this theatergram at length through Beccari's, Andreini's, and Guarini's plays ("*La castità conquistata*," 316–20).

[24] Ray points out that in Beccari's play, while Stellinia is trapped by the satyr, Turico,
the shepherd in love with her, forces her "to vow her love for him" before he consents to
free her from the satyr's trap ("*La castità conquistata*," 316). In spite of Melidia's cunning
escape, Beccari's story has the traditional conclusion.

Satiro's vows set up Scene Two to be an enactment of the usual damsel-in-distress theatergram. Andreini, however, turns the tables on tradition. Filli is not the typical beloved who blushes or swoons. Instead, she is a nimble thinker and a fast talker who rescues herself with the finesse of an accomplished con-artist — or perhaps, a courtesan.

Filli first tricks Satiro into believing that she wants him as much as he wants her, then convinces him to let her tie him to a tree, ostensibly because she is afraid that his overly ardent embrace might smother her. The satyr agrees to be tied up, and the situation immediately becomes more sexually charged. Satiro's eagerness, however, begins to wane when he realizes how tightly he is being bound. Filli tells him that the more securely she ties him, the better she will kiss him afterwards (1397–1401), but when she begins jerking him around by the beard and pinching his breasts (1435–1443), he finally understands that his plan to torture her has been turned upon himself. "Baciamo presto, che farem la pace" [Let's kiss quickly, then make peace] (1447), he suggests nervously. Filli, however, is not certain that he has learned his lesson. She insists that she wants this experience to be beautiful for them both and feigns amazement that he does not care for her caresses. Next Filli tricks him into eating an allegedly sweet, but actually very bitter herb to sweeten their kiss. He tastes it and cries, "Ohimè, che cosa è questa / cotanto amara?" [Oh me, what is this thing so bitter?] "O malaccorto," she retorts, "or hai pur finalmente conosciuto / ch'io mi beffo di te . . . ?" [O imprudent one, . . . have you at last understood that I am making fun of you . . . ?] (1484–1485; 1488–1489). Having rescued herself from a dangerous situation and thoroughly rebuked Satiro for his reprehensible intentions, Filli calmly walks away, with his pitiful cries for her to untie him ringing out behind her. Soon after, Satiro swears off women and love and vows to become a follower of Bacchus (3.3.1668–1669).

Andreini's satyr scene is perhaps more reminiscent of Beccari's scene with Melidia or Guarini's scene with the wicked Corisca (*Il pastor fido*, 2.6) than it is of Tasso's classic version. Beccari, however, uses the scene to give a comic twist to a scenario that he will later conclude in the traditional way with Stellinia's capture, and Guarini uses it to illustrate Corisca's evil, wily nature (her golden wig flies off, and the satyr accuses her of witchcraft), while for her part Andreini uses it to emphasize Filli's intelligence and ability to protect her own honor. Neither a helpless damsel nor a scheming villainess, Andreini's character defies these stereotypes. Of course, as the actress herself surely realized, her manipulation of the theatergram created a surprising and comic turn of events that audiences would love, not to mention a star turn for a character that they would long remember.

With the figure of Ardelia, Andreini lampoons not the damsel in distress, but the classic Petrarchan beloved. In doing so, she alters the myth of Narcissus. In the fourth act, Ardelia, the haughty, chaste follower of

Diana and Uranio's obsession, falls ardently in love with her own reflection while bathing in a spring (4.4). Love-struck, she vows to accept the reflected woman as her goddess (2515), but in vain she reaches out to touch her and strains to hear her voice. Ultimately, she curses her own tears, for they cause the water to ripple, and she realizes that they deprive her of seeing herself (2586–2590). Doglio views Ardelia's fascination with her reflection as an image of lesbian erotica, and the sensual richness of Andreini's description in this scene may easily be read to support this theory. I would also argue that this scene especially provides a subversively wicked and witty interpretation of how narcissistic the stereotypical Petrarchan beloved might prove to be, if that paragon described in male-authored poetry were more fully developed as a character. Andreini, it seems, realized that taking the stereotype to its limits — the usual chaste, cold, awe-inspiring beauty — and then pushing things a bit further by allowing her to speak would produce in essence, a caricature, a creature so self-absorbed that she even falls in love with herself. This deviation from tradition would surely have struck a chord in her audience, who would have been a bit shocked, perhaps, but amused at the same time.

Ardelia's scene inspired by the story of Narcissus may illustrate the ways in which Andreini's experience with the *commedia dell' arte* provided her with additional inspiration for the composition of her play — or her play may have inspired *commedia dell'arte* pieces. Richards and Richards point out that although the extant *scenarii* "provide a major source of information about commedia dell'arte performance, ... they are fraught with interpretative difficulties. Most can be dated only approximately, their provenance is diverse and often uncertain, and they exist in various states from the skeletal to the more elaborate" (*Commedia dell'Arte*, 141). Because of these difficulties, it is hard to say exactly in which direction influence may have run, but a glance at K. M. Lea's "Specimen Scenari" reveals several pastoral *scenarii* that contain theatergrams reminiscent of those in *La Mirtilla*. One three-act play called *Li Tre Satiri*, or *The Three Satyrs*, seems particularly related to *La Mirtilla*. In it, a character called Filli "discourses on hunting, the power of the Magician, and her deliverance from his enchantments. She says that she is weary and rails against love and describes the bliss of those who follow Diana" (*Italian Popular Comedy*, 666). She falls asleep beside a fountain, and, in order to punish her, the Magician enchants the fountain so that upon awaking and seeing herself in it, she will fall in love with herself (667). Such tantalizing similarities call for further investigation into the connections between *commedia dell'arte* and *commedia erudita* in Andreini's work.[25]

---

[25] Dating the sketch is somewhat difficult. Lea notes that *Li Tre Satiri* is recorded in *Della Scena de' Soggetti Comici et Tragici di B(asilio) L(ocatello) R(omano)* "in two parts 1618

Another scene in *La Mirtilla* that deviates from the Tassian prototype is the one in which Filli and Mirtilla, both in love with Uranio, decide to compete in a singing contest[26] to see which one is worthy of him. A similar situation arises in *Il pastor fido* in which both Corisca and Amarillis are in love with Mirtillo; there, however, Corisca plots Amarillis's death to put an end to the competition (3.1). In *La Mirtilla*, Opico, the wise old shepherd appointed judge of the contest, prudently declares Filli and Mirtilla "pari ne la beltà, pari nel canto" [equals in beauty, equals in singing] (3.5.1790), and he advises them to make peace between themselves, for Uranio loves no one but Ardelia. The two women see the wisdom of his advice and swear to value each other and their friendship over their infatuations with Uranio (1810–1826). Doglio suggests that this scene illustrates "la saggezza delle donne" [the wisdom of women] (13). The valuing of female friendship over romantic relationships is clearly an instance of deviation from tradition, one that deprives the audience of such moments as that in *A Midsummer Night's Dream* when Helena and Hermia temporarily dissolve their friendship amid accusatory cries of "canker-blossom" and "puppet" as they square off over Lysander (3.2.282, 289). Yet, Andreini boldly risks a new scenario for this situation — one that is equally entertaining, allows her to show off her musical talent, and underscores her appreciation of the importance of female friendship.

Concerning Andreini's breaks with tradition, Doglio notes that *La Mirtilla*

> abbandona il gioco di travestire da pastori esponenti della società di corte, così mescola all'idillio pastorale l'idillio gastronomico, all' amore, alla seduzione, al sottile erotismo delle ninfe e pastori le gioie del pane e del vino, gli stimoli della fame, la voglia di satollarsi. ("Introduction," 12–13)

---

and 1622" and that the MS is in the Biblioteca Casanatense, Codices 1211 and 1212. She also notes that it may be found in *Raccolta di Scenari piu scelti D'Istrioni Divisi in Due Volumi* and that the MS is in the Biblioteca della Reale Accademia dei Lincei in the Palazzo Corsini, Rome, Codices 45G. 5 and 6. Finally, she records that it is reprinted in F. Neri's *Scenari delle maschere in Arcadia* (Città di Castello, 1913).

[26] Regarding the music that would accompany the singing in *La Mirtilla* and would be an integral part of the performance of the play, MacNeil points out that for both *commedia dell'arte* and *commedia erudita* plays, "music was seen as an aspect of a play's performance rather than its composition" so that unless "it is directly specified within the dialogue of a play that a character or characters are to sing, there is usually no indication of the drama's musical content" ("Life and Work," 106–7). She does discuss, however, existing primary sources that indicate some "rules and guidelines" for incorporating music, including Angelo Ingegneri's *Della poesia rappresentativa e del modo di rappresentare le favole sceniche*, ed. Maria Luisa Doglio (Modena: Edizioni Panini, 1989), in which he discusses "the inclusion of choruses and *intermedii* in tragedy, comedy, and pastoral dramas, as well as ... the theoretical justifications for inserting music at various moments in a play" (107).

[abandons the game of disguising shepherds as representatives of the court, as it mixes with the pastoral idyll the gastronomic idyll, love, seductions, the subtle eroticism of the nymphs and shepherds, the enjoyment of bread and wine, the stimuli of hunger, the desire to satiate it.]

Far more than a vehicle for playing out the pastoral fantasies of nobles, *La Mirtilla* is rather a movable feast for the celebration of the many facets of love. The rich variety of love and desire that Andreini depicts in the play is indicative of her astute understanding of the human experience, as well as her ability to argue philosophically about the nature of love. Amore and Venere's framing commentary on Amore's ability to manipulate the fates of lovers and his plans to ensure their perfect obedience encompasses the following: Uranio and Tirsi's debate about love and free will (1.1); Ardelia, Mirtilla, and Uranio's stichomythic show of *sprezzatura* (2.3) in which they provoke, insult, and attempt to bribe each other regarding their respective loves and hatreds; Gorgo's paean of praise to the joys of eating and drinking, in which he argues that Bacchus and Ceres are far more worthy of worship than Venere and Amore (3.3);[27] Mirtilla and Filli's contest in which friendship wins over infatuation (3.5); Opico and Tirsi's debate regarding the pleasures of the hunt versus the pleasures of love (4.1); Coridone and Tirsi's debate on the merits of understanding nature and the seasons versus the merits of love (4.2); and Ardelia's passionate blazon of adoration for herself (4.4). Fortunately for her audience, Andreini offsets the rigorous debate format of some of these exchanges with consummate comic skill.

When Tirsi is finally persuaded by Coridone's smooth rhetoric that love is perhaps something he should try, he immediately stumbles across the lovelorn Mirtilla. Just as passionately as he previously argued against love, he now marshals his powers of persuasion to make a conquest. Unfortunately, he hasn't had a lot of experience. After an awkward start in which he attempts to convince her how learned, well-born, athletic, and rich he is, Mirtilla gently responds, "Comprendo dal tuo dir, gentil pastore, come tu sei d'Amor nuovo seguace ..." [I understand from what you say, gentle shepherd, that you are a new follower of Amor ...] (2427–2428), and she goes on to refuse him as delicately as possible. When he still hasn't taken the hint, by the beginning of Act Five, she resorts to a resounding, "... ti prego per Dio che omai tu lasci / cotesta tua si vana e

---

[27] In Andreini's depiction of Gorgo, we see traces of the gluttonous Arlecchino, further illustrating the playwright's blending of elements from the *commedia dell'arte* and the *commedia erudita*. For more information, see Lea on connections between Arlecchino, the Zanni, and their love of food (*Italian Popular Comedy*, 62, 73–88).

pazza impresa. / E se meglio aggradire / mi vuoi, partiti omai." [... I beg you for God's sake that you give up for good / this vain and crazy enterprise of yours! / And if you really want to please me, / get out of here!] (2691-2694). The extreme reversal of Tirsi's attitude toward love, combined with his virgin efforts at seduction, are matched in their capacity as comic relief by such scenes as Ardelia's attempts to draw nearer to herself, and her cursing of the waves in the spring as she does so: "Onda tu sei / nata per cagionar la morte mia: / onda ben credo che l'origin hai / da Flegetonte, poiché per tua colpa / tutt'avvampar mi sento;" [Wave, you were / born to cause my death! / Wave, I do believe that your origin was / Phlegethon,[28] since from your blow / I feel myself burst all into flames!] (4.4.2535-2539); and Satiro's torture by Filli, along with his subsequent, ignominious rescue by Gorgo (3.2; 3.3). Clearly Andreini's experiences with *commedia dell'arte* helped her develop a strong sense of comic timing.

Throughout, Andreini's language is colorfully descriptive sixteenth-century Italian, full of Petrarchan conceits and loaded with intriguing disclosures of her knowledge of hunting, botany, and agriculture, as well as her copious knowledge of mythology. In Act Four, Tirsi and Opico discuss the intricacies of hunting birds with subtly hidden nets (4.1.1910-1926) and bird calls (1961-1970); then Tirsi and Coridone describe the importance of knowing when to prune the grapevines, how to graft them, and when to gather them, as well as when to shear sheep, how to milk them to make cheese, and how to tend the fields (4.2.2130-2153). For all of these there are *exempla* in Latin pastoral poetry.[29] For almost every idea she introduces, Andreini provides *exempla* from classical mythology and ancient history for authority. One of the most extensive catalogues of examples is found in the Prologue, where Venere lists many famous couples for whose tragic fates Amore has been blamed (lines 18-54). When writing of food, nature, or geography, she also includes mentions of the classical world. She drops references to "le crude tigri ircane, / i leoni superbi di Nemea, / e di Lernea le velenose serpi" [the cruel Hyrcanian tigers, / the proud lions of Nemea, / and the poisonous serpents of Lernea] (1.262-264) as easily as she does to Bacchus, Ceres, Proserpine, or Cynthia. In spite of her subversions, adaptations, and general flaunting of her knowledge and talent, however, Andreini carefully maintains the boundaries of Renaissance tragicomedy.

To cast the shadow of tragedy over her comedy, Andreini has some characters concur with Coridone's argument that lovers should be willing

---

[28] Phlegethon was one of the rivers of hell, mentioned by Virgil and Seneca in descriptions of the underworld. Its waters were on fire.

[29] See, for example, Virgil's *Georgics*.

to confront death for their beloveds (4.2.2248–2251). Near the end of the play, Ardelia, still sighing for herself as she gazes at her own reflection, hopes to end her fruitless longing in death (4.4.2595–2604). Igilio, fearing his love for Filli will never be reciprocated, decides to stab himself to death (5.2.2730–2741), and Tirsi threatens to throw himself down a ravine when Mirtilla refuses him (5.1.2695–2699). Although such threats introduce the requisite possibility of a tragic ending, Doglio points out that in the fifth act, "L'atmosfera di turbamento, di passione lesbica, di amore impossibile e doloroso si dissolve" [The atmosphere of anxiety, of lesbian passion, of impossible and sorrowful love dissolves], and the disharmony gradually dissipates in the dialogue between the couples ("Introduction," 14). Ultimately, Mirtilla and Filli save their lovers' lives by deciding to accept their proposals, and Uranio convinces Ardelia to divert her love from herself to him, using the classic *carpe diem* approach (5.5.2872–2881). His cunning description of the effects of time — her "dorate chiome" [golden hair] becoming silver and her "polita guancia" [polished cheek] becoming crinkled and faded—work wonders on her attitude (5.5.2872–2878).[30] When she does decide to love him, however, he notes with timeless sexism that she has clearly proven herself a woman, since she so quickly changed her mind, and he rejoices that "il bel femineo sesso / ... possiede ... il consiglio / più saggio quanto men pensato" [the beautiful feminine sex / ... possesses ... counsel / even more sage than thought] (2909–2916). Upon considering Uranio's attitude, one realizes that Ardelia's punishment may not quite be over. Finally, as is traditionally the case with tragicomedies, there is a happy ending. The play concludes with all the contented couples making offerings of thanksgiving at the temple of Venere for the lessons they have learned. The individual questions about love debated throughout the play are subsumed in the end in the group acknowledgment of Amore's power.

In 1973, Robert L. Erenstein opined that *La Mirtilla* is "far from the worst" of the "numerous pastorals written in those days" ("Isabella Andreini," 43). I would argue that in many ways *La Mirtilla* is one of the best: it strikes a novel balance between *imitatio* and *contaminatio* of the traditional theatergrams used in pastoral tragicomedy.[31] Furthermore, it provides a female-authored counterpart to such canonical standards as

---

[30] In her description of the aged Ardelia, Andreini also seems to participate in the burlesque tradition, painting a portrait of a woman that is completely at odds with the traditional Petrarchan ideal. For a discussion of this tradition, see Maria Galli Stampino's article "Bodily Boundaries Represented: The Petrarchan, the Burlesque and Arcimboldo's Example," in which she discusses the "mocking portrait of the old woman" (65–67).

[31] See Clubb on the use of imitation and contamination regarding the structure of theatergrams (*Italian Drama*, 5–6, 11).

those by Tasso and Guarini. While scholars have long argued the merits of works by male playwrights who imitate or at least pay homage to *Aminta*, they have been slow to recognize the contributions of female playwrights to the pastoral tragicomedy.[32] For example, Elizabeth Story Donno traces the progress of the Renaissance pastoral tragicomedy through a series of male authors, printers, and translators to show the historical as well as the creative process through which the tradition passed en route from Italy to England,[33] yet her commentary excludes discussion of both *La Mirtilla* and Wroth's *Love's Victory*. Clubb, too, omits *La Mirtilla* from a list of twenty male-authored Italian plays that she surveys in her chapter, "The Making of the Pastoral Play," mentioning it only in her commentary on Andreini at the end of *Italian Drama in Shakespeare's Time*. A play printed and reprinted as many times as *La Mirtilla* is deserving of more than just a historical note regarding its existence.[34] It should be explored within the contexts of Renaissance literature and drama, as well as women's literary history. Above all, the play is an arch, amusing romp that will appeal to students and teachers of Renaissance literature and drama as they explore the fascinating developments of playwriting from this period.

THE TRANSLATION

My goal for this project was to render a text that is a close translation of Andreini's vocabulary, being mindful of her sixteenth-century idiom, while at the same time producing an easily readable, standard English text, suitable for use in the college classroom. Although Burton Raffel scorns the translator who would "chop one Rabelaisian sentence into five," arguing that such an editorial decision "is about as false a representation as can be" (*The Art of Translating Prose*, 106), I must confess to altering the occasional lengthy Andreinian sentence — usually one that is a long series of clauses strung together with semicolons — into two or three sentences at the most. While Andreini and her publishers clearly counted on readers and actors to provide dramatic expression, emphasis, and pauses according to their natural instincts and understanding of the rhythm of the words, as well as the contexts of the speeches, I have taken the liberty of using standard

---

[32] For a discussion of Andreini's and Wroth's contributions to this subgenre of drama, see Julie D. Campbell, "*Love's Victory* and *La Mirtilla* in the Canon of Renaissance Tragicomedy," *Women's Writing* 4 (1997): 103–24.

[33] Preface and Introduction to *Three Renaissance Pastorals*, ix–xxxiii.

[34] It is listed as no. 50 in Mauda Bregoli Russo, *Renaissance Italian Theater* (Florence: Olschki, 1984), 18–19, citing "Isabella, Comica gelosa," in *Studi e documentazioni del Teatro Stabile di Torino* (Milan: Mursia, 1971), no page given.

English punctuation. I have, however, endeavored to avoid skewing Andreini's meanings or emphases with my use of punctuation, and, when in doubt, I left well enough alone.

The primary text on which I have based this translation is Doglio's 1995 edition, which in turn is based primarily on the 1588 edition, published in Verona by Sebastiano dalle Donne and Francesco Compagni.[35] I have also consulted the subsequent reprint of this edition from April of 1588, as well as the 1599 edition published by Francesco dalle Donne and Scipione Vargnano in Verona and the 1605 edition published by G. Bordoni and P. Locarni in Milan. Doglio's text mainly deviates from the 1588 edition in that she modernizes the Italian spelling and regularizes the capitalization. Her text retains for the most part the line breaks of the original, and I have attempted to keep similar placement in the English. For the sake of making comparisons between the English and Italian texts, I have followed Doglio's system of line numbering, although there are a few discrepancies in that system.

---

[35] Unfortunately, there do not seem to be any extant manuscripts of *La Mirtilla*.

Isabella Andreini
La Mirtilla: A Pastoral

DEDICATION

To the most illustrious and excellent Signora, the lady
Lavinia de la[1] Rovere, Marchesa del Vasto.

My most revered Signora,
    I began almost as a joke, most illustrious and excellent Signora, to
apply myself to the study of poetry, and I found it such a delight that I
have never since been able to give up such entertainments. And, although
heaven denied me the genius suitable for so high and noble an exercise, I
was not thereby dismayed; on the contrary, I strove to be like those who
are born and reared in the snowy Alps or sterile fields, who nevertheless
struggle with all their might to cultivate the land and produce something
as fruitful as possible. Human genius is a thing too divine, and those who,
reckless in their idleness, allow such a rare gift to perish do not deserve to
be counted among humankind because they, passing their lives in perpetual
silence, in the same way that the animals do, are good for nothing but con-
suming that which nature or the earth has produced. From this way of life
and [these] customs I wished to distance myself, so I followed instead the
studies I had begun. In doing so, I found myself, in days past, composing
a pastoral which I, perhaps too bold, now send out with the escort of your
most illustrious and excellent name, desiring that it help me to show you
the devotion and reverence which I bear to you, but not intending that the
authority of your divine name defend my work, for, since this is the first
labor of my talent brought to light, I desire to listen freely to the opinions
of everyone, in order to amend the defects of this work, as well as of my
other writings.
    Accept, therefore, Your Most Illustrious Excellence, this my pastoral
that I now present to you, with the same kindness that many times you
have deigned to show, against my every merit, lending agreeable silence to

---

[1] In Doglio's edition, we have "de la." In the second printing of the 1588 edition, we
have "della," and in the 1599 edition, we have "de la." The variations seem to be the work
of the printers for each edition.

my lively words. And, so as not to inconvenience you, humbly I bow to you, kissing with every reverence your worthy hands and praying to God for your every great pleasure and happiness.

From Verona, 24 February 1588
From the most humble and devoted
servant of Your Most Illustrious Excellence,
Isabella Andreini, Comica Gelosa

INTERLOCUTORS

Amore and Venere	Speak the prologue
Uranio, a shepherd	In love with Ardelia
Igilio, a shepherd	In love with Fillide[1]
Coridone, a shepherd	In love with Nisa, who does not appear in the play
Tirsi, a shepherd	A hunter
Opico, a shepherd	An old man
Filli, a nymph	In love with Uranio
Mirtilla, a nymph	In love with Uranio
Ardelia	A nymph of Diana
Satiro	In love with Filli
Gorgo	A goatherd

---

[1] Andreini uses both Fillide and the short version of this name, Filli, to refer to the same nymph. In this edition, I shall use Filli hereafter in the names that mark the parts. In 5.2.2719, Igilio uses her full name, which I retain.

PROLOGUE

*Amore and Venere*¹

Venere	Truly, it is granted to me, beloved son,
	to find you again! Now tell me, for what reason
	did you leave the bosom of your mother?
Amore	In truth, I enjoyed sweet repose
5	in your beautiful bosom, up there in the third heaven,²
	and happy I lived, for I had left
	in the world fire, beautiful and holy,
	so that my gift to the human race,
	to the wild beasts, birds, forests, and waves
10	might be divided and scattered. [Yet,] while
	I expected to receive immense praise
	in recompense from mortals, I heard
	from frantic lovers
	both quarrels and complaints!
15	So that the relentless and mournful voices
	would no longer disturb my ears,
	I descended to earth to pacify their
	vain and troubled minds.
Venere	O dear son,
	why is it that loud complaints
20	are always brought against you? Everyone calls you
	a murderous tyrant, wicked and deceitful!
	They say that you are the sole root of scorn and fury,

---

¹ Amore and Venere may be translated as Cupid (or Love) and Venus. I retain the Italian versions of their names as characters in the play, just as I do for all the other characters.

² In the Ptolemaic system, the third heaven is that of Venus, as it also is in Dante's *Paradiso*. See Doglio, *La Mirtilla*, 161. Petrarch, too, refers to the "terzo cielo" in his sestina, poem 142, "A la dolce ombra de le belle frondi ..." (*Canzoniere*, trans. Musa 230).

cruelty, pain and shame,
and that from you suspicions
25   are born, [as well as] injuries, betrayals, wars,
frauds, rebellions, deceptions, and deaths!
I also hear it said, to your shame and scorn,
that because of you Pyramus and Thisbe
were made miserable and sad by their ardent loves,[3]
30   and the swimmer of Abydos ended up
a victim of the sea, and his unhappy lover
from Sestos ran to follow him in death.[4]
They add that because of you miserable Halcyone and Ceyx
lost their lives,[5]
35   and the Greek lady
left her grieved spouse, whence burned ancient Troy;[6]
and sorrowful Phyllis, having in vain
awaited Demophoön, finally, deprived
of hope, ended her life with a noose.[7] [What's] worse,
40   they also say that because of you burned
the incestuous and unbridled ardor
of Myrrha for her father[8] and the infamous
fraternal flame of Byblis and of Canace;[9]
and that only because of you was Medea cruel;[10]
45   and Scylla cut her own father's

---

[3] Pyramus and Thisbe were star-crossed lovers of Babylonia. They died because Pyramus, believing Thisbe had been killed by a lioness, killed himself, and, upon finding him dead, Thisbe stabbed herself with his sword.

[4] Leander of Abydos drowned swimming the Hellespont to meet his lover Hero of Sestos, who was a priestess of Venus.

[5] Halcyone, the daughter of Neptune, was married to Ceyx, who drowned on his way to Clarus to consult the oracle of Apollo.

[6] Helen, wife of King Menelaus of Sparta, was convinced by Paris to elope to Troy with him, causing the eruption of the Trojan War.

[7] Phyllis, the lover of Demophoön, a son of Theseus, hanged herself when Demophoön seemingly scorned her and did not return from Athens after the appointed time.

[8] Myrrha, daughter of Cinyras, king of Cyprus, had an incestuous affair with her father.

[9] Byblis, daughter of Miletus and Cyane, or possibly Eidotea or Area, fell in love with her brother, Caunus. When he did not return her ardor, she killed herself. Canace, daughter of Aeolus and Enarete, and lover of Poseidon, fell in love with her brother, Macareus. She seduced him, conceived, and attempted to hide the baby after its birth, but Aeolus allegedly threw the baby to the dogs and sent a sword to Canace. Both she and Macareus killed themselves.

[10] After being spurned and abandoned by Jason, Medea killed their children, burned down their palace, and fled to Athens where she married King Aegeus.

blond, fatal hair.[11] Pasiphaë
because of you alone gave birth to the horrendous monster
that was the shame and burden of her womb,[12]
and Hercules, who once supported the stars,

50   held the distaff and turned the spindle:[13]
and more I would say, but modesty closes
my mouth, so I do not speak of Tereus[14]
and Semiramis,[15] or of so many other
infamous and dishonest incidents!

Amore   Know, beloved mother,
that a dark veil so encumbers the minds
of miserable mortals,
that they do not see the cause
of so many of their misfortunes, nor do they observe how

60   it is not Amore, but a fury who offends them!
While I was far away from you
I dwelt unrecognized among them,
in order to unburden myself of these false accusations,
and I exposed to them this wicked rascal,

65   who, by taking my form,
always deceives them,
having the boldness, that rash and impious fellow,
also to call himself the son
of Venus and Mars,[16]

70   as if heaven could have produced so wicked a seed!

---

[11] Scylla, daughter of Nisus, king of Megara, fell in love with her father's enemy, Minos. In the myth, Scylla cut off her father's blond locks, which were the source of his strength, causing him to lose the war against Minos. Minos, however, held Scylla in great contempt and rejected her love, so she threw herself either from a tower or into the sea, depending on the story.

[12] Pasiphaë, wife of Minos, King of Crete, fell in love with a bull, which was a gift from Neptune meant for sacrifice, and she gave birth to the Minotaur.

[13] Omphale, daughter of King Iardanus of Lydia and widow of Tmolus, ruled her husband's kingdom. A powerful woman, she was able to buy Hercules when he was sold as a slave by Mercury. Hercules allegedly became so enamoured of Omphale that he was willing to dress in women's clothing and spin wool, while she wore his lion's skin.

[14] Tereus was married to Procne, but raped her sister Philomela and cut out her tongue, so she couldn't tell what he had done.

[15] Semiramis was a queen of Assyria who was renowned as a strategist and a warrior, but she also was known for her licentious affairs, and she developed an incestuous desire for her son, Ninyas, son of Ninus, king of Assyria.

[16] Different traditions exist concerning the parentage of Amore, or Cupid, the god of love, but one of the main stories states that his parents were Venus and Mars.

The liar was born of lust and idleness
and then nourished on vain thoughts:
He pretends to be Amore
in order to deceive people, armed with both a bow
75   and quiver! I do not know how
he has even formed wings and flies, and in everything
feigns my figure; except
I have eyes and see,
while he has eyes but is completely blind!
80   Everywhere I spread my celestial fire
and nectar, the rascal slips in;
concealed by disguises,
he pours out his venom, and with false
dispositions he destroys them! Promising
85   long peace and comfort, he first attracts them
with false pleasure; then, when he has drawn
them to his will, he keeps them trapped
always between fear and hope, and he feeds them on sorrow.
Then, these desperate ones he leads to death!
90   This is that cruel enemy of pity,
who always longs for tears and always
rejoices in evil while I nourish myself with goodness.
He brings dubious joy and certain grief,
while I give my pleasures
95   both true and certain and with sweet ambrosia
feed the soul! In summary, I am Amore,
and he is a blind error who kills
reason and abandons the reins to blind sensuality!

Venere   O ignorant minds of mortals,
100   who believe that this fury, who has neither goal
                nor moderation,
is Amore, and yet surely they must at least
perceive your followers,
which are truth, prudence, and faith,
fear, honor, true contentment and peace,
105   honesty and steadiness,
along with secure hope,
the wise and holy pleasure of chaste fire,
with which the torch of Hymen burns.[17]

---

[17] The chaste fire of Hymen, god of marriage, refers to married love.

	Yet his abominable followers
110	are errors, rages, hatred, scorn,
	furies, frauds, lies,
	insanity, unbridled daring,
	desperation, deceit, war and death!
	He, even if he has wings, flies to the ground,
115	never rising up, and his strength fails
	when mortal beauty fades.
	But you with your wings carry your followers
	to heaven, and time cannot damage
	your powers, nor can death itself,
120	because you do not love fleeting beauty,
	but that [beauty] which is celestial and divine. And what need have I
	to speak more of the inequality
	between you? I can sum it up in only one statement:
	You alone are the life in this life
125	of every created thing, and he is the death!
	But I rejoice, because you have made clear to them
	what your powers are, what you yourself are:
	so that from now on Amore may always be called love,
	and no one will attribute to you
130	that which the crazy and errant fury
	produces among mortals. Amore will be praised
	as a true guardian of the people,
	and a giver of joy and pleasure!

Amore	You know, my mother, that it was always
135	my law and custom
	not to allow my faithful followers
	to perish,
	but to punish
	those who proudly scorn my powers.
140	Now know that while returning
	to see heaven again,
	I paused my flight for a while in this place,
	where, with great sorrow and astonishment,
	I heard myself blasphemed and scorned
145	by an arrogant shepherd named Tirsi
	and by a nymph called Ardelia.
	This time I will stop here to punish them, and when
	they are most rebellious against me,
	and when they least expect it, I will make them repent

150	of their temerity! You, dear mother,
	stay with me in these woods until
	a suitable outcome conforms to my will.
	Here we will be invisible among them,
	and, when it is time, their hard hearts
155	I will prick with this golden arrow;
	then one will burn and not be requited
	for the love of Mirtilla, and the other will blaze up
	in great pain for love of herself!
Venere	Are you perhaps offended
160	by these senseless ones
	who have not realized
	the power of the gods?
	You perhaps wish to have harsh revenge upon them?
Amore	That would be an effect contrary to my being,
165	if I, Amore, hated loving
	and desired revenge such as only hatred,
	my enemy, desires! It does not suit
	me, who am Amore,
	to give way to wrath, for that frequently
170	extinguishes my great fire.
Venere	Then what will happen to them, beloved son?
Amore	After Tirsi has fully understood
	my worth and no longer has hope
	of possessing Mirtilla, who of Uranio
175	is enamored, and despises and scorns all others,
	I will permit their fury to induce them to
	desire escape from their pain through death:
	but, because I do not ultimately consent
	to others' deaths, I will take away the power
180	of my enemy and have Mirtilla submit
	to [Tirsi's] desires. I will not have her love
	Uranio, who flees her to pursue
	Ardelia, who, her love for herself spent,
	will become Uranio's bride.
185	I will then have Igilio,
	longing to do violence to himself,
	raise by this means great pity in the beautiful bosom
	of Filli, for which she will completely

abandon Uranio and give herself only to Igilio.
190   And Coridon will always be happy
with his Nisa, because they were always
devoted to me. And thus I will have satisfied
the divine laws
of my great kingdom!

Venere   Then let's do these things, beloved son,
and amuse ourselves here in the
woods nearby until it is time
to carry out whatever you desire.

Amore   O my mother, if these marvels
200   are heard by some fool,
they will be believed fables; yet in truth
they will surely be true!
For [mortals] don't know what heaven can do,
and that to make
205   a disaffected heart become loving,
and to make another fall in love with herself,
are not miracles to the highest gods,
who can do whatever they want!

Venere   Yes, son.

ACT ONE
SCENE ONE

Uranio and Tirsi, shepherds

Uranio 210	Bright sun, whenever you come out from your damp bed, will you not find me as miserable and sad upon your return as I was upon your departure? O iniquitous stars, O hostile fate, you plot my misfortune! Whenever were
215	so many miseries gathered in one sole breast?
Tirsi	He who yields to his suffering, as you do, should complain only of himself and not of others. You are the cause, Uranio, of your own injury and of your continual worry.
220	You foolish man, you only want to end your days miserably!
Uranio	Just as I did not elect to love the one who hates me, I cannot stop following her!
225	She, ungrateful, always flees me, and by fleeing, destroys me. Too happy is that shepherd who can love or not love whenever he wishes!
Tirsi 230	Our will is like that liquor which gives life to a small burning flame: for if it is missing, it follows that the flame is missing, too. Now if you desire that your great fire end, do not give it any more nourishment.

Uranio   How can I ever rule my desires like that?

Tirsi   Free is our will, and one may desire
              freely that which he wants, in spite of Amore.

Uranio   It is true, Tirsi. I also confess
              that our will is free, but when
              Amore lives in our hearts
240   with a thousand and more roots
              entwined,
              he so greatly oppresses us
              that our reason
              is very weak, and one can do almost nothing!
245   The cruel flatterer so lures us
              that we live happily
              in martyrdom and pain. How we can
              free ourselves we scarcely know!

Tirsi   Flee, so that by escaping Amore, you conquer him!

Uranio   And where shall I flee? To heaven, perhaps?
              He lodges in heaven and makes tremble
              even thundering Jove and the other eternal gods.
              In the air, perhaps? He takes to the air
              in flight, and with his torch
255   ardently inflames the simple birds.
              Perhaps you will say that in some impenetrable wood
              I could attempt to hide myself.
              Don't you know that there is no wood
              so horrid and thick,
260   that he does not penetrate it
              with his lively fire? It is true:
              the cruel Hyrcanian tigers,
              the proud lions of Nemea,
              and the poisonous serpents of Lernea,[1]
265   and many wild beasts roving through the forests
              claim it clearly and undoubtedly,
              often fighting for Amore.
              In the deep ocean I would perhaps escape him?

---

[1] In Lempriere's *Classical Dictionary*, the town is spelled "Lerna" or "Lerne." The reference is to the Lernaean Hydra, the multi-headed serpent.

	Alas, even the fish, although in water,
270	have no defense against his great fire!

Alas, even the fish, although in water,
270 have no defense against his great fire!
You cannot suggest anything to me, my dear Tirsi,
other than I go among the damned spirits.
Alas, not even there might I yet find escape
from the lad who conquers all the world,
275 since the king of the Averno lakes,
burning for Proserpina,[2] shows us
that even in his kingdom it isn't possible to flee
Amore's great power. And what more certain
sign may one have of his strength,
280 than if he doesn't wish to pardon
his mother and himself?
Therefore you must believe that in vain one attempts
to flee his hand,
since not only in heaven, on earth, and in the sea
285 does he show his immense power,
but also with his great valor
this invincible and tremendous deity
miraculously invades the inferno!

Tirsi   You foolish lovers! You
290 fancy him a god
so that you may have a worthy excuse for your shortcomings!
Don't you know that the gods, miserable and foolish one,
govern justly over all, yet he
always rules his kingdom unjustly?
295 Amore is none other than a blind fury,
a hurtful good, an insecure support,
an unjust tyrant to the bottom of your hearts.
The goodness that he shows you is a sham, and the evil
unfortunately is true; and if he occasionally
300 promises something good, soon he deprives you
of the hope of enjoying it; thus, the greater
the pain, the more your anguish increases.
These are the pleasures and the contentments
that you experience in loving:
305 for a trifling pleasure,

---

[2] Pluto, king of the underworld Avernus, was so enamored of Proserpina, daughter of Jupiter and Ceres, that he carried her away to the underworld where he made her his queen.

a thousand grave torments,
and for a little sweetness, much bitterness.
Never do you experience a blessing
without torments and pains!
310   Thus, I can easily say that every pleasure
that Amore has you taste is none other
than a fleeting delight and a steady sorrow,
a dubious good, a certain evil,
a concealed honor, and an obvious dishonor,
315   a faith perfidious and frail,
a prompt fury, tenacious and strong,
a lazy reason, a sensuality swift and nimble,
an uncertain joy,
and a most certain torment!

Uranio   Blind, blind is the mind of those
who say that Amore
is not a powerful god!
If he were not, how could he
keep one devoid of heart alive for many years
325   and make him die to himself
and live in another?
To be more where he loves, than in that place
where he dwells? And finally, what
greater certainty could one ever have
330   of his divinity, than that serving him
we care not for ourselves?

Tirsi   O miserable butterfly,
you fly around your internal flame,
and you desire with blame and injury
335   to end your life! Surely you could
make happy your days
by obeying me and abandoning Amore:
but if it pleases you to be a lover,
love the beautiful Filli,
340   who (alas!) longs for you,
and stop pursuing
(if you still want me to call you shrewd and wise)
Ardelia, who flees you and everyone else.

Uranio   Certainly I would sooner
345   die for Ardelia

than delight in another,
who is less beautiful.
Don't you know, Tirsi, don't you know
that Ardelia, for whom I always burn, is so beautiful
350   that she leaves everyone who beholds her
full of astonishment and wonder?
She has locks so blond and bright
that they make the sun's rays envious and ashamed!
Her brow is of privet,
355   and of roses are her cheeks. Of coral
are her beloved lips, and the whiteness of lilies
is conquered by her even and well-formed teeth.
Of ebony are her arched and precise eyebrows;
her eyes are so clear and lucid that they
360   easily surpass the sun! Her neck is so round and white,
that beside it milk loses its whiteness; her breast is made
of pure ivory with two unripe apples
that may be seen to tremble under a veil
as she exhales from that sweet mouth
365   her exquisite breath, to which
fragrance yield the winds
that come from Arabia!
And between the two little valleys of snow,
where her beautiful mouth is confined,
370   rests Amore with his tinder and flint,
hidden there in the opening,
now this heart, now that one
sweetly enflaming!
Long and round are her beautiful arms,
375   long [is] her white hand.
Her body is of frank and virtuous measure,
her leg straight and slender,
her foot small and elegant.
But what shall I say of her glances, which
380   the scarcer they are, the more powerful
they are to enflame the soul with burning ardor?
Her words then are so shrewd and wise
that they cannot be heard without one's heart
remaining caught and conquered!
385   But where do I leave her laugh,
which, whenever it appears
between her rosy lips,
makes me see paradise on earth?

	Hence, I judge Ardelia,
390	very full of beauty,
	but without pity!

Tirsi	You unhappy lovers judge
	not by following truth, but by following
	blind affection, which causes you to serve
395	a cruel and false nymph.
	But since so courteous
	I have found you, in having me know
	of your nymph's many beauties,
	for pity's sake also reveal to me
400	when you fell in love with her and how
	you were caught in her amorous trap.

Uranio	I would not know how to deny you a thing so just!
	When we shepherds,
	in beautiful flowered April,
405	crown the flocks
	with verdant branches,
	and place over the door a wreath,
	richly adorned with flowers and fronds,
	everyone likewise crowns with beautiful flowers
410	his herd and flock;
	and with smoke of pure sulfur he walks
	around the animals,
	to remove their every possible affliction.
	Then we adorn all the yokes and the plows,
415	the plowshares, the hoes, and also the rakes
	with sweet-scented flowers,
	while we make
	the cottages resound
	with sonorous pipes. Then all
420	the animals appear content,
	as do the wise shepherds,
	for the solemnity of so great a feast,
	a sacred feast every year
	for Pales[3] our goddess.
425	Then, as I say, I was made
	the prey, alas, of Amore,

---

[3] Pales was the goddess of sheepfolds and pastures.

and this happened while I was going to the sacred temple,
where we gathered
for worship around a venerable, old priest,
430   adorned in a white robe
and crowned with a green garland.
With a joyful face
and pure and holy zeal,
he turned to the east
435   and killed a pure white lamb,
throwing its hot entrails
on the fire, that burning there
carried to heaven with its flame the odors
that the rich Arab land
440   gathers from the prosperous Sabean[4] trees.
Then, bowing to earth
on knees pious and reverent,
he turned his eyes to heaven,
and asked for our pardon from the divine Pales,
445   if, out of misfortune or folly,
either we or our herd
had disturbed any meadow, fountain, or forest
consecrated to her, and with the same voice
he asked for mercy and a gift:
450   that a charm, a lightning bolt,
a witch's art, [or] the evil eye,
never could disturb
our woolly flock and herd.
And, with pious accent
455   he prayed that she would watch over our dogs,
[over] their faithful escort, so that the milk,
wool, and beautiful offspring
would always be abundant, and never
would some of us return
460   weeping and mourning
with the bloody skin
of a sheep, a goat, or a bullock
taken with anguish from the mouth of a greedy wolf,
but that upon our return in the evening to our lodgings,
465   our herd's number would be just as it was

---

[4] Saba was a region in Arabia that was famous for frankincense, myrrh, and aromatic plants.

when we had departed at the break of day.
When this ended, we came out of
the sacred temple, and in a beautiful group we saw
many nymphs gathered in a lovely meadow.
470   Leisurely, they
were gathering pretty flowers.
Among them I saw Ardelia,
alas, and I may say
that the instant I saw her, I burned for her!
475   And I burned even more for her
when I heard that she lamented
with her companions
the cruel death of the innocent lamb
sacrificed that day.
480   Then I said to myself: "If she mourns so
for an animal, that was offered in sacrifice
for the honor of Pales,
what would she do upon seeing
a man who would die for her?"
485   Certainly, I said, I will find her as kind
as she is beautiful. And then fixing
her beautiful suns
in my desirous eyes,
and flashing in sweet laughter, it appeared
490   that she wanted to confirm everything!
I was so moved by this
and by that beauty, which has no equal,
[that] I resolved to love her!
Already the sun has passed four times
495   by the twelve houses[5]
since the day she enflamed me
and tied this wounded and burned heart of mine
in sweet knots
with her golden locks.
500   Now you have heard
the full story of my misfortune.
I did not think it excessive for me to recount to you
these solemnities that I undertook,
when I was a sad victim of Amore,
505   since I know that six days before,

---

[5] These are the twelve signs of the zodiac.

in leaping over a great ditch, you fell into it,
striking your foot on a stone,
and so great was your blow
that many days after,
510   you remained injured:
so here you are told in full
that which you did not see.

Tirsi   It means a great deal to me
to hear about what I did not see, and from your account
515   I have clearly understood how
in a fine way indeed
Amore lay in wait for you,
and in an even more opportune way,
he easily made you become his servant.
520   But I fear that since you caught fire
in the season that only produces flowers,
you will thus have only flowers
for your long service!

Uranio   O, if among so many flowers
525   I could have that flower which I so greatly covet,
I would call myself happy!
But perhaps such a miserable shepherd
is not allowed to hope for so great a blessing.

Tirsi   So sweetly you speak, Uranio,
530   that I didn't notice
that while I listen to your words
and talk with you
about love, a voracious woodworm
in your miserable heart,
535   the hours pass swiftly, and I do not go
to my usual pleasures:
therefore, I leave you. Good-bye, and stay in good spirits!

Uranio   I want to come with you! Wait, Tirsi,
who knows, perhaps by coming with you I might
540   see the no less cruel
than beautiful Ardelia!

SCENE TWO

Filli, nymph

Filli   Sometimes I think about
      my formerly happy state which was equal to any other's,
      and now more than any other's
545   it is weary and full of tedious worries!
      Then sorrow afflicts and vexes me,
      and desperation induces me (alas)
      to desire death.
      O, Filli, more unfortunate than any other!
550   You surely know, O forests,
      valleys, woods, and fields,
      what my life is like, because so often
      you hear me complain, and the winds also
      know, for, listening to my sharp pain,
555   they often pause.
      Then I, so unfortunate — while the stars
      decorate the beautiful night sky,
      and Cynthia[6] alights in the embrace
      of her beloved youth, and the night
560   spreads its dark veil,
      and sleep and silence
      offer tired mortals
      their deserved repose — I go out alone
      without fear of a horrid encounter
565   with nocturnal ghosts. Miserable and lost
      in the lonely forests and desolate fields,
      I call to Uranio in vain. When I demand of
      heaven if it will always be so unmerciful to me,
      Echo, who always responds to my speech
570   from the rocky hollows, increases my torment.
      Thus I disturb the night of its faithful silence
      with solemn cries of woe, and while I cry,
      I hear night birds, whose screeching
      brings me a sign of bad luck.
575   And living in such death, I see the stars
      vanish one by one, until only

---

[6] Cynthia is another name for Diana, the goddess of the hunt, who is dedicated to chastity. The "beloved youth" is Endymion, a shepherd whom Diana loved in her guise of goddess of the moon.

the amorous star remains in the sky.
While it belatedly departs from me,
I humbly pray that it puts some end
580   to my misfortune; otherwise, I
will become a bitter Parca to myself.[7]
And while I speak thus, she flees,
scorning my prayers. In the meantime
lovely Aurora rises from the sea,
585   her dewy locks bound with roses.
When heaven paints beautiful flowers
and cheerful things the most,
in my sad heart
the fierce pain greatly increases,
590   for it appears to me that as much
suffering as the world holds
is all harbored in this miserable soul!
Thus, entire nights and days
I consume in pain and weeping.
595   Once the leafy woods,
the warbling of the birds,
the murmur of the springs,
the sweet susurration of the light winds
among the green locks of the myrtles and laurels,
600   and the agreeable and beloved odors
of the flowered land
carried to my heart total sweetness,
but now nothing helps me.
Through long experience (alas)
605   I have become aware, O pitiless Uranio,
that my misfortune pleases and nourishes you,
and yet you hope that I die! My death
pleases you more than the elms
with their twisted branches.
610   You also know, cruel one,
that the morning roses do not love
the dew as much as Filli

---

[7] The Parcae (Fates) were the three powerful goddesses believed to preside over the life, death, and fortunes of each human being. Clotho, the youngest, presided over one's birth, holding her distaff. Lachesis, the middle sister, spun out the actions and events of one's life, and Atropos, the eldest, cut the thread of life with scissors. By declaring that she will become a Parca (Fate) to herself, Filli indicates that she will enact the part of Atropos by cutting her own life's thread, thus committing suicide.

loves cruel Uranio!
Therefore my weary eyes will always pour forth
615   bitter weeping, and my sad mouth
will heave ardent sighs from my mournful heart
until I in misery reach my final hour.

SCENE THREE

Filli, nymph, and Igilio, shepherd

Igilio   Neither more beautiful rays from serene eyes
nor a whiter hand, nor more golden locks
620   have ever burned, captured, and wounded a free heart
than those by which I was,
my sweet Filli,
burned, captured, and wounded!
Filli, nothing more beautiful than you
625   could Amore show me in his kingdom,
and whoever longs to see
the torch of Amore, his bow and arrows,
and Venere with her Graces, and ultimately
all the beauty of nature united together,
630   must admire the sweet mouth and lovely serene regard
of you, my Filli:
and then let him live, if he can, without sighs.
I envy the grass, the rocks, the flowers, and the branches,
that are touched by her, and I long always
635   to change myself into a flower, not only to adorn
her tresses or her delicate breast,
but also to catch her grace and her scent.
Oh, if I were grass or a stone that was
touched by her white foot one day,
640   I would defeat with joy every other lover!
And if I became a leafy branch,
that for her jest or sport
by her soft hand was touched,
I would be completely happy and fortunate!
645   Ah, if I could transform myself into a tree
so leafy, that she, scorning any other,
would come to rest in my shade,
I would not envy
the famous plane-tree,

650   that made shade for Europa and the great Jove.[8]
                    Oh, if I could become a spring,
                    [yet] not losing by this my human sense,
                    and that you, my Filli,
                    would come to refresh your beautiful limbs
655   in my waves, the spring that often sees
                    Diana nude would not be able
                    to equal the joy
                    of my happy state!
                    But if I could not transform myself into a flower, grass,
                        a stone,
660   a branch, a tree, or a spring,
                    might I at least change myself into a wild beast,
                    a wild beast that by you
                    would perchance be pursued,
                    because if forbidden things make
665   our desire grow,
                    then I would flee from you,
                    only to induce in you a greater desire
                    to follow me and finally take from me my life,
                    and very happy I would be,
670   if that white and delicate hand
                    cut the thread of my mortal life.

Filli   O pitiless Amore! Here is he who
                    by your fault loves me,
                    and I because of you, alas, cannot
675   give him such faith in return!
                    To increase my pain, I am condemned
                    to loving him who hates me and to serving him who does
                        not prize
                    my faithful service and my love.

Igilio   O lucky me, here she is now!
680   Without transforming myself into another form,
                    I see my beloved Filli!
                    Here is the beautiful flame that undoes me —

---

[8] Jove took the form of a bull to entice Europa. He then carried her on his back to Crete, where he seduced her. In some versions of the story, they were shaded by a plane-tree. This detail appears in such sources as Pliny's *Natural History*, XII.v, and Theophrastus's *Enquiry into Plants*, I.ix.3.

I will draw near and say:
Have pity on my languishing!

Filli   I will pause here, for I see
that he burns with desire to speak with me,
and I want to show him the same pity
for his misfortune that I would like
another to show for my sorrow.
690   Well I have learned, alas, at my own expense,
to show myself courteous!

Igilio   Most kind Filli,
have pity on me, your unfortunate servant!

Filli   If by our works
695   one may see our hearts,
I believe that you know, Igilio, how much
I deplore and regret not being able
to give for your service the mercy you deserve,
but I cannot dispose of those things
700   that through the fault of Amore are no longer mine.
I belong to another and cannot be yours
because I am not even my own.

Igilio   How can it be, that we have love in common
but do not share the desire
705   that he with his torch lights in us?
Yet somehow it is true, and with my misfortune I prove it,
O sweet lodging of my every thought!
Force yourself and grant to me
part of your grace, so that Amore
710   does not go about proud of the grave pain
that each one of us sustains. Remember
that everything is abundant in the world,
except for innocent and unfeigned lovers —
and since you know in me as much faith
715   as there is beauty in you, do not wish that I
reap from my love so sad a fruit!

Filli   With you I can mourn your misfortune,
but I still cannot, as much as I would like,
give you courteous aid. O fierce destiny!
720   I would like to help you, but I do not know how!

Igilio   You see, charming Filli,
                   my misery is so great that I
                   feel even greater suffering
                   upon seeing you sympathetic to my misfortune
725   than I would if you were cruel to me!
                   So, my heart, cease being merciful
                   in so fierce a way!

Filli   Do not be displeased, Igilio, that I show you
                   the tenderness of my heart, and be grateful
730   that I, not being able to love you, feel sorrow.
                   No longer desire of me that which I cannot do!

Igilio   I thank you for your courteous kindness,
                   but since death comes out of this clear
                   dazzling light from which life should come forth,
735   I can easily say, alas,
                   that the pity you bestow is cruel to me,
                   but never will my harsh fate make it so
                   that I don't love you like life itself.

Filli   And I must beg you,
740   not to regret that I
                   cannot give you the reward
                   of that love which you say you bear for me:
                   therefore, take my advice again, O dear friend,
                   and like a wise man remedy your misfortune!
745   I, if it pleases heaven to make me free,
                   would well have you know
                   that, just as I advise you in one thing,
                   I would happily satisfy you in the other:
                   but I cannot stay with you
750   any longer, Igilio,
                   since these eyes of mine seek their
                   sweet food and gentle nourishment.
                   I leave, therefore, to see if Amore
                   wants to be as merciful to my desire
755   as he was to yours. Remain in peace.
                   I go to see if I may
                   speak, as I have done many times,
                   with my cruel Uranio,
                   but I pray that my fate
760   will grant me the grace to find him

changed from his usual way.

Igilio   Go freely, Filli, my heart, go where you wish!
              I pray to Amore and heaven
              that he shows himself favorable to your desires.
765   Miserable Igilio, in what destiny are you?
              Would you long that Filli
              find Uranio piteous to her pain?
              Alas, now he hates her and flees her,
              and she follows him and loves him; but what is to be, then,
770   if it happens that he does not flee her but loves her?
              Which part will remain of Filli's heart
              that can be Igilio's? O me! How I fear
              that if he is caught one day in her beautiful eyes
              and hears her sweet words,
775   he will become a lover! Then, Igilio,
              you will be deprived of every hope; then you will see
              your beautiful nymph in the breast of another.
              May heaven not keep me alive
              to see such a vexing prospect!
780   May death first close these eyes with his hands
              so that I will never see
              what makes my heart freeze
              in my breast and the blood in my veins,
                   if I only think about it!
785   But that blind youth, who enjoys so much
              the discordant will that he observes in two hearts,
              perhaps will make Uranio
              burn for another nymph and scorn Filli:
              I will not remain deprived of hope!

End of the First Act

Ardelia, nymph

Ardelia	Now that the hills and valleys are adorned with jewels
	of white, vermilion, blue, and yellow flowers,
	I will sit by this clear spring
	that, with its sweet and pleasing murmur,
	invites me to rest my weary limbs,
795	and weave a pretty garland for my hair,
	so that everyone will admire Ardelia's flowers.
	And, with invariable thought, they will observe
	my modesty so very dear
	to the chaste goddess
800	who with her beautiful light illuminates the shadow
	and silvers the fields and forests
	dedicated to her. Now I sit: Oh, what beautiful flowers!
	I may well compose a garland so
	beautiful that my friends will envy it!
805	But, since I feel rather tired
	after following a roebuck
	who emptied my quiver of arrows,
	I must first yield these eyes to the mercy of Sleep.[1]
	Courteous god, tranquillity of the world,
810	repose of the living, friend Sleep,
	I pray you, leave the Cimmerian grottoes[2]

---

[1] Somnus, or Hypnos in Greek, was the god of sleep and the brother of Thanatos, death. He lived in a dark cave where the sun never shone.

[2] Andreini uses "cimerie," or Cimmerian, to indicate that the caves are dark and gloomy. The Cimmerians were a mythical people who inhabited a land of darkness, swathed in perpetual clouds. In Book Eleven of the *Odyssey*, Homer describes the abode of the Cimmerians near the opening of Hades. Andreini is again making reference to the dark cave or caves of Somnus.

where happily you sojourn,
and come to alight in my eyes.
O faithful companion
815   of your friend the night, come
close my eyes,
for your faithful friend Silence
happens to be with me. Here the bull doesn't bellow,
the goat doesn't bleat, and the dog doesn't bark;
820   here the wolf doesn't howl,
here the cicada doesn't shrill,
here the frog doesn't croak,
here the bird's song doesn't announce the day.
Here nothing is heard
825   but the murmur of this clear spring,
which almost mimics the sound
of the shepherds' zithers at night,
as it breaks so sweetly among the rocks.
Alas, if kind heaven never denied you
830   your charming wife, grant me
sweet repose.[3] Don't you know how many, many
times in the diurnal hours you have given me
what I now ask of you?
With dear oblivion spread anew, then,
835   my eyes, and with your black wings[4]
cover me completely, because far more precious
to me when I am weary is your darkness
than that clear light I now see.
But foolishly, while I speak
840   I interrupt the silence,
and, since without it you can do nothing,
I had better be quiet! O winds,
O trees, O rocky caves, where Echo
lives, repeat nothing
845   of what you have heard.

---

[3] In Book Fourteen of the *Iliad*, Hera bribes Sleep (Hypnos) to lull Zeus to sleep by promising him one of the Graces, Pasithea, for his wife. She then seduces Zeus, and Sleep, disguised as a bird of night, puts him to sleep. Sleep then tells Poseidon to aid the Greeks as they fight against the Trojans while Zeus slumbers.

[4] Somnus is often portrayed lying on a bed of feathers with black curtains, with his son Morpheus nearby, to make sure that nothing wakes him. Morpheus, also considered a god of sleep and dreams, is usually represented as a corpulent child with wings. Andreini's "black wings" echo the image of Somnus's black curtains and the feathers of his bed, as well as Morpheus's wings.

Dear friend Sleep,
here is the arm I place
on the grass, and on the arm I lay my head,
so that soon you will give me
850   the usual repose.

Scene Two

Ardelia and Mirtilla, nymphs

Mirtilla   Having already put the bridle on his lithe war-horses,
blond Apollo had sprung from the bosom of Tethys,[5]
Aurora[6] was already driven away, and the highest
    mountain peaks
were becoming gold,
855   when, eager for new flowers,
I went out from my faithful lodging.
And, sitting in a meadow at the foot of a hill
from which descended a stream so brisk and pure
that it appeared to be
860   liquid silver, running swiftly
into winding channels throughout that meadow
adorned with a thousand flowers, a thousand,
birds delighted me with their sweet song.
And in the midst of such pleasure,
865   I saw (O me), I saw Uranio,
who was leading his white flock
to a nearby pasture. As soon as
my eyes saw him, my heart
was left wounded and burnt! Then instead
870   of gathering flowers, I gathered nettles and sticks,
and instead of perfumed roses
I put sharp thorns in my bosom.
It was you alone, Uranio,
who bound my soul

---

[5] Tethys was a sea deity, the wife of Oceanus. Tethys is also used poetically to refer to the sea. Apollo was the god who drove the chariot of the sun across the sky.

[6] Aurora was the goddess of the dawn. She is usually represented in a rose-colored chariot, being drawn across the sky. She set out before Apollo in his chariot and was the forerunner of the sun's rising.

875   in a stubborn knot,
             when sweetly
             with your skilled reed pipe you accompanied
             your dulcet accents to which, while
             your woolly and fat flock grazed
880   on the dewy short grasses,
             unhappy Echo responded from these rocky caves!
             From then on, I have never known peace.
             On the contrary, in sighs, complaints, and burning flames
             I always suffer under this my heavy burden.[7]
885   Amore, the root of all my misfortune, never
             gives me the strength and vigor
             to reduce such ardor.
             Although my eyes always shed
             bitter tears, they do not put out
890   even in part the amorous fire.
             My sighs forbid it, for their wind
             always rekindles the flames with greater strength.
             Thus I consume my tired life;
             thus all becomes a flame to the fire,
895   all wind to sighs, all water to weeping;
             thus, bitter tears
             will always pour from my eyes,
             sighs from my mouth, and fire and flames from my heart.
             Ah, my sweet Uranio, come to her
900   who so prizes and loves you! Come at last
             to her who adores you, to the one who scorns
             anything she sees, except your beautiful eyes!
             What proof of my steadfast faith, ungrateful one,
             do you have left to try, left to see?
905   Alas, why to my prayers
             are you so pitiless?

Ardelia   O me, what mournful sound
             disturbs my sweet, gentle repose?
             Mirtilla, is it you who laments, bringing forth
910   from deep in your heart such sorrowful accents
             and fiery sighs?

---

[7] Mirtilla's "grave spoglia" or "heavy burden" is her mortal body.

Mirtilla   I am she, who is more melancholy
than the mournful souls who have lost the day.[8]

Ardelia   Perhaps this happens to you because you love too much?

Mirtilla   Alas, it is quite true
that each of my torments
is caused solely by Amore.

Ardelia   O wicked and impious son of Venere,
who with perpetual pain
920   fill the minds and hearts of those who
foolishly give faith
to your empty promises!
In all these complaints
I read, unhappy lover,[9]
925   a clear and notable sign, that in following you
one finds nothing other than pain.
This enemy flame of mortals
burns, destroys, and consumes every pleasure!
Thus, I judge to be without reason
930   whoever follows him.

Mirtilla   O gentle Ardelia,
do not be so arrogant
as to allow yourself to offend
the invincible son of the goddess Venere!
935   Don't say that those who follow him
are deprived of judgment, for perhaps
one day you might become his servant.

Ardelia   Sooner the ancient chaos will return[10]
than in me will ever be harbored thought of love!
940   And if I, to my misfortune,
ever became subjected to him,

---

[8] Andreini writes "l'alme dolenti che han perduto il giorno," which may also be read as a euphemism for "the mournful souls who have died."

[9] The "infelice amante" or "unhappy lover" is Mirtilla.

[10] Andreini echoes Ovid, *Metamorphoses* 2.299. See the discussion of her appropriation of this term in the Introduction, xiv.

> my triform goddess,[11] my great Cynthia,
> of him a fierce enemy,
> would soon deliver me from his hand.

Mirtilla   O foolish one, don't you know that she
> couldn't free herself?
> Endymion[12] can attest to this,
> who was by her so hotly loved,
> and Pan, god of the shepherds,
950   who for a fleece of white wool
> cordially took her into his arms.[13]
> Therefore, do not brag that
> you can resist him because the most proud
> and pitiless hearts he has conquered and tamed —
955   but do you not see, Ardelia, here is my sun!

Ardelia   Whom do you call your sun?

Mirtilla   That shepherd who is the sun to my eyes:
> clear sun that melts me,
> that descends from that hill —
960   do you see him yet, Ardelia?

Ardelia   Certainly, I see him.

Mirtilla   He is my sun!

Ardelia   What are we to do?

Mirtilla   I want you to hide
> behind that oak,
> if you long to serve me, and I will stand
> behind this elm.

---

[11] Diana had three forms: the moon in the sky, Diana on earth, and Hecate in the underworld.

[12] Endymion was a shepherd who requested that Jupiter grant him eternal youth and the right to sleep as much as he wanted. Diana is said to have seen Endymion naked and asleep on Mount Latmus (a mountain in Caria, near Miletus), and she was so struck by his beauty that she began descending from heaven every night to be with him. See also Act One, note 6.

[13] Pan gained Diana's favor by turning himself into a beautiful white goat.

Ardelia	And then?

Mirtilla	Listen carefully!
965	You see how quickly he comes toward us,
	so I want us to be hidden and quiet
	until he arrives. If he speaks,
	we will wait and listen.
	Do not reveal yourself
970	until I do; then if he
	desires to chat with you, as usual,
	pretend to scorn him.

Ardelia	I say that truly
	I will scorn him because I've always scorned him
	as a fierce enemy of my well-being,
975	but why do you want this?

Mirtilla	Because I hope
	that your cruelty and my faithfulness
	will make him change his mind and desire.
	Here he comes! He is already near us —
	let's hide ourselves quickly!

Ardelia	Here I hide!

Mirtilla	And here I stand! Gentle Amore,
	grant me that this day be
	the end of my misfortune, the beginning of my well-being!

SCENE THREE

Uranio, Ardelia, and Mirtilla

Uranio	[to himself] Tirsi may think, do, and say whatever
	he wants, but he will never
985	take from me my love! O me, only death could accomplish
	that;
	and if one still loves after death,
	not even its strength would have the power
	to extinguish into oblivion this flame of mine,
	which so sweetly consumes me,
990	that I boast and brag of burning and languishing!

I know that the beauty of my goddess
is such that Amore has placed in her his nest,
and with his hand weaves
from her blond tresses the dear knots
995 with which he ties the hearts of a thousand lovers!
Her eyes and her brows are
his arrows and his bow
that he never shoots in vain;
her wide forehead
1000 is the pass through which he entices his victims;
her rosy lips are the flames
with which he always burns
each cold heart;
her ivory breasts
1005 are his strong prisons, and he himself
is her prisoner, having been conquered,
and thus increasing my beautiful
Ardelia's glory and pride.
Therefore it follows that he
1010 has no power against her;
thus, she lives joyfully and kills others,
and of other people's pain she laughs and boasts.

Mirtilla [to herself] O sorrowful Mirtilla!
You have truly heard anew
1015 the cause of your misfortune,
but I pray, my suffering, that in such a war
you will give me some truce! Peace I don't ask,
because a miserable lover
is not allowed to ask so much,
1020 yet I desire to make myself bold
to help myself.
[to Uranio] Heaven make you happy,
O dearest part of my soul!

Uranio Happy I would be if I didn't see you.

Ardelia I also will reveal myself,
to see the one for whom Mirtilla longs.

Uranio I seem to hear the voice of her
whom I love and honor!
And here she is! Oh, how fortunate! Whenever

1030   did I see her that she did not scornfully turn
             her feet elsewhere? For as long as I've loved her,
             I have never seen so much pity
             for my martyrdom! Since she is not leaving,
             and appears to want me to speak to her,
1035   I will approach her boldly!
             [to Ardelia] Well met, sustainer of my life!

Ardelia   I would sooner sustain
             all the martyrs of the world
             than support you.

Mirtilla   Look, Uranio, listen to me, for I love you as much as
             the silent fish love the seaweed and the waves!

Uranio   Look, Ardelia, listen to me, for I love you as much as
             the ingenious bees love beautiful flowers!

Ardelia   Shepherd, leave me be, for I hate you as much as
1045   the bleating sheep hate the wolf!

Uranio   Nymph, leave me be, for I hate you as much as
             the birds hate the sticky traps!

Mirtilla   Spring does not have as many colors
             as there are tortures
1050   that torment my soul for you!

Uranio   Not as many flames shine in the heavens
             at night as there are ills
             that because of you I suffer continuously!

Ardelia   Not as many birds fly in the air,
1055   as there are irritations
             that I feel for you when I see you and hear you!

Uranio   Not as many arrows flings Amore,
             as there are torments
             that you with your detested appearance give me!

Mirtilla   The greyhound follows the wolf; I, alas, follow
             you, who flee me and with your fleeing kill me!

Uranio   The wolf follows the sheep; I, alas, follow
             the blessed and dear tracks of your feet!

Ardelia   The doves flee the birds of prey,
1065   and I flee your sight!

Uranio   The fearful hares flee the dogs,
             yet much more I flee and hate Mirtilla!

Mirtilla   If you accept me as yours, I will give you
             a veil whereon you will see in the beautiful work
1070   miserable Adonis's fierce death,[14]
             and you will see infuriated Venere, who,
             to avenge her lost love,
             sends Amore's little Cupids to the woods,
             and it seems that she says, "Bring here captive
1075   the pitiless, ferocious beast, so that I may
             pour forth against it my irate heart."

Uranio   If you accept me as yours, charming nymph,
             I will give you a bow adorned with gold
             whereon you will see, engraved by a skilled hand,
1080   Hymen with polished and beautiful cheek,
             crowned with various purple flowers.
             He holds in his left hand a purple veil
             and in his right, burns a lamp.[15]
             And you will see it so beautiful and well composed,
1085   that it would seem a spirit, having voice and speech.

Ardelia   If you will leave me alone for good, Uranio,
             I will give you my faithful Torrent,[16]
             who among my beloved dogs
             is the dearest and most welcome.
1090   Indeed, he justly carries

---

[14] Adonis, out hunting in the woods, was mortally wounded by a wild boar. Venus, who was passionately in love with Adonis, tried to save him but could not, so she changed him into the anemone.

[15] Hymen, the god of marriage, was usually depicted as being crowned with flowers and holding a torch in one hand and a vest of purple in the other. Note that a bow, associated with Cupid, is decorated with an image of the god of marriage. These offerings of gifts in wooing are a staple of pastoral poetry.

[16] "Torrente" could also be translated as "Stream."

the proud name of "swift torrent,"
for there is no wild beast in these woods
so fleet and quick that
he, running, does not stop or capture it,
1095   either in the forest or on the mountain or plain.

Uranio   If you will stop bothering me for good, Mirtilla,
I will give you a vase where on one side you will see
Jove transformed into a swan
who is happily nestled in the breast of his Leda;
1100   on another side you will see that for Callisto
he has taken from Diana her face and her clothes.
On yet another side you will see him changed into an eagle
for the beautiful Ganymede,
and finally, for Danae, you will see him changed into a shower
of gold.[17]

Mirtilla   Where were you born? On a mountainous cliff?
Did the Hyrcanian tigers give you their milk?[18]

Uranio   Pray, were you born among the frozen mountains?
Were you delivered, cruel one, of a lioness?

Ardelia   Pray, were you born of a deaf asp[19]
1110   since you will not hear me? I say that I hate you!

Uranio   Pray, were you born to annoy me
and goad me always? I say that I hate you!

Mirtilla   O stronger than marble to my great weeping!

Uranio   O colder than snow to my great fire!

---

[17] The illustrations on the vase depict Jupiter's transformations in order to seduce mortals. Leda, the queen of Sparta, gave birth to Pollux, Helen, Castor, and Clytemnestra, each a set of twins who sprang from the eggs resulting from this union. Callisto, the daughter of the king of Arcadia, and a servant to Diana, gave birth to Arcas and was later transformed into a bear. Ganymede was taken up to heaven by Jupiter as he was hunting, and he became the cup-bearer to the gods. Danae gave birth to Perseus.

[18] An allusion to Virgil, *Aeneid* 4.365–367, where Dido berates Aeneas, crying, "False one, no goddess was your mother, nor was Dardanus founder of your line, but rugged Caucasus on his flinty rocks begat you, and Hyrcanian tigresses suckled you."

[19] An allusion to Psalm 58.4, ". . . they are like the deaf adder that stoppeth her ear."

Ardelia	O more annoying than the strident cicada!
	Remain in your misery! Yet I leave
	so that I no longer have to listen to you or look at you!

Uranio   Ardelia, you flee me and perhaps believe
            with your flight to have me
1120   finish my days,
            but your thought is in vain,
            because your image that stays here with me,
            even if you steal away from me,
            keeps me alive.
1125   Neither distance nor time
            can make me stop loving you,
            for one cannot take from the heart
            what can be taken from the eyes.
            Alas, if some compassion for my grave sufferings
1130   may arise in your chaste breast,
            and if hope ever owes faithful service
            some mercy, take pity on me! Turn,
            turn [upon me] those clear lights
            that have burned my heart with lively fire!
1135   Ah, if your beautiful fleeing soles
            were pierced by thorns, what pain
            would it cause me? Stop, then,
            your foot too swift to my injuries!
            Don't leave my eyes
1140   deprived of their light,
            for with continuous weeping
            they will irrigate my afflicted cheeks and breast.
            You alone can save my life,
            that already runs quickly
1145   towards death! Oh, I am not
            yet so disfigured that you have to flee from me,
            pitiless Ardelia! Here I keep for you, listen,
            a white deer, a goat, and a wolf
            accustomed to being in the same den
1150   with my faithful Melampo and Lisisca,[20]
            and contrary to his nature
            he plays with the sheep and the lambs.
            If this is not enough, I promise still

---

[20] Melampo and Lisisca are Uranio's dogs.

	to make a sacrifice to you as my goddess,
1155	and to make Arabian odors rise in smoke from the altars.
	Oh, if pitiful prayers have power over you,
	do not flee me, cruel one, do not deny me
	so sweet a sight, alas, for which I breathe!
	Oh, if to passionate faith
1160	passionate pity owes hope,
	surely my faith should
	hope for some mercy;
	but you, who never in your heart
	have received love,
1165	scorn my misfortune and rejoice
	to see me languishing.
	Yet, O me, I am compelled to follow you!

Mirtilla	Oh, why do you pursue, Uranio, the one who flees you?
	Oh, why do you flee, Uranio, the one who pursues you?
1170	Why do you love the one who hates you?
	Why do you hate the one who loves you?
	Oh, why do you prize, miserable lover,
	a cruel lady who scorns you?
	Oh, why do you scorn, unkind beloved,
1175	a faithful lover who prizes you?
	Oh, flee the one who flees you,
	scorn the one who scorns you!
	Welcome the one who pursues you,
	give love for love, hate for hate.
1180	Will it ever be possible for you to yield
	to such just prayers?
	Don't you see that the stars,
	the air, the water, the earth,
	and the most proud winds
1185	in the long run change their style, place, or temper?
	You alone, like hard rock,
	always remain rigid and immobile —
	but why did I say "rock"?
	For to the waves of the sea
1190	rock sometimes gives way,
	and a small drop may burrow into it.
	But you, ever more firm
	in your fierce desire, O me, remain;
	sometimes life, sometimes death the stars show,
1195	neither in one color does the earth always dress,

nor does the ocean always appear disturbed;
the winds are sometimes angry, sometimes benign.
And all other things
are sometimes favorable or sometimes averse,
1200   but your rigid heart
in perpetual tenor of cruelty
stays the same for me! You always flee me,
you always threaten my life with death:
ultimately, cruel one, every thought,
1205   every word, every deed,
and all that you think and say and do,
is only to give me an early death!
But, be it as it may: I will follow you.

End of the Second Act

ACT THREE
SCENE ONE

Satiro

Satiro   Already in the expanse of heaven
1210   four and six times the luminous moon
              has filled its silvered horn,
              and as many [times] has waned and emptied it,
              since the day that pitiless and cruel Filli
              put my neck in the yoke of love.
1215   Filli, Filli, truly you have a heart of stone
              and thoughts of wind! More stinging
              than nettles you are to me, pitiless Filli,
              Filli, so ungrateful, Filli!
              I will ever shout out over these mountains
1220   that you are cruel to me and that, although cruel to me,
              so much more from my heart I love you, my heart!
              And if what I say isn't true, I pray that heaven
              strike me dead right before your
              beautiful eyes that I love so much!
1225   But what good is it to me, alas, to swear to you,
              if you pay no attention to what I say?
              O unwelcome Amore, at least return to me
              the dear liberty that you have taken from me!
              Now, fleeing the heat, the shepherds
1230   rest in the shade, the grazing flock
              continues munching grass, and the little birds
              upon the branches sing of their loves.
              And for you, in the hollow grottoes,
              the snakes have no poison,
1235   and the wild beasts have no savagery.
              And in the grassy bottom of the swift
              and transient rivers,

the flickering fish are happy,
and under the trees

1240   the beautiful nymphs are playing in the shade
with wanton wood sprites and shepherds.
And you, cruel one, flee me, and perhaps,
in pursuing fugitive beasts in the hunt,
your tender and delicate soles grow weary.

1245   Tell me, nymph, no less foolish than beautiful,
what good is it always to have your heart in the forests?
At long last, take repose in these arms!
But perhaps you scorn these limbs
because they are robust, hairy, and hard?

1250   Don't you know that this is really our gift?
For just as you nymphs are as beautiful
as you are delicate, we, then,
are as handsome as we are rough.
You must not disdain these goat-like

1255   feet, for with them every swift
beast I can outrun, and if the lofty horns
of this high forehead displease you,
remember that in the sky the beautiful moon
also has horns, and nonetheless

1260   was dearly loved
by our rustic and half-goat god.[1]
Bacchus also has horns, and Ariadne
burned with love for him, scorning every other.[2]
If you dislike the redness of these cheeks,

1265   notice, my dear, that even the moon itself
grows red when it appears in the east,
and when the wind threatens us, the sun
is equally red when it rises from the sea
and again when it plunges into the sea.

1270   If you also despise this hairy coat,
know, my sweet dear, that Alcides unconquered
by a horrid lion
often wore its coat, and for him Deianira

---

[1] The moon reference is to Diana, the moon goddess, who was loved by Pan, the half-goat god of shepherds and hunters. See also Act Two, note 13.

[2] Bacchus, the son of Semele and Jupiter, taught people to cultivate grapes for wine. He is often depicted with horns. He married Ariadne after she was forsaken by Theseus.

was all ablaze with amorous fire.[3]

1275   Filli, do not scorn me! Come, for a gift
you will have the head and the branched horns
of an old stag! Come, my divine sun!
But you do not care for my gifts, nor do you care
that I am (alas) for you some fog in the wind.

1280   But if love avails nothing, I will try deceit!
I will stand behind that bush,
and if she, as is her custom,
will walk through this meadow,
with my arms I will make a chain,

1285   and, if she won't surrender to my will,
I'll do her a thousand outrages!
Neither her beauty nor her loud cries
or her request for mercy will help her!

SCENE TWO

Satiro and Filli

Filli   It would perhaps appear to some that I am worthy
1290   of every grave punishment for not loving
him who loves me. I don't deny it, but what can I do
if Amore doesn't want me to think or do anything
unless it pleases him?
Cruel Amore, you alone make every face

1295   vile and cowardly to me,
except the beautiful image of him
who makes my life bitter and sweet!
Well I know (alas) and well I realize
that the pain I do not express

1300   is far greater than
the one I voice,
but remedy, my heart, with pity
for the misfortune that all comes
from your cruelty!

1305   How much better is it to praise you
as the giver of life

---

[3] Alcides is another name for Hercules. He is often depicted wearing the skin of the Nemean lion. He married Deianira, the daughter of Oeneus, king of Aetolia, who decreed that she could marry only the strongest of all her suitors.

	than to blame you
	as the one who denies help?
	What excuse can you find in your defense,
1310	my Uranio, unless you believe
	that slaying others is worthy of great praise?
	I do not ask you for anything else
	but that you regret my pain
	and that now and then you listen to my laments.

Satiro   There, I have you! Now you can't escape!

Filli   Oh me! What is this I hear? Who grabs me?
          Who does me violence?

Satiro   Ah, pitiless one,
          it will no longer profit you to be cruel,
          nor will running like
1320   the swiftest of winds!
          From here you will not depart unless for my sufferings
          you give some recompense.
          And if, ungrateful one, you do not wish
          to give my burnt heart some refreshment,
1325   I will tie you naked to that hard oak,
          where with torture you will end your life!

Filli   Mercy, oh mercy,
          goat-like god! First
          listen to my prayers!
1330   Alas, what glory is there
          in conquering a nymph
          who is already overthrown by your beautiful eyes?

Satiro   [aside] You see how she mocks now if I get angry?

Filli   I swear by your robust arms
1335   and by your charming horned brow,
          that I do not mock you, nor do I wish to mock you!

Satiro   So, Filli, you love me and want to give me
          a fitting reward for my faithful service?

Filli   Certainly I love you! What nymph could ever see you
1340   and not burn for you? I believe you are such

that she who sees you and then doesn't love you
must be made of Caucasian stone!

Satiro   And why, foolish one,
                have you remained silent and appeared to me
1345   disagreeable and cruel?

Filli   This I did
                to test you, my sweet life.

Satiro   What sign could you give me that this is true,
                and that you reason in your heart as you do in your words?

Filli   If you command me, then you will see
1350   that I speak to you with good judgment, and you will find
                the results of your commands far greater
                than my words and promises alone imply.

Satiro   [aside] For this first time,
                I will feign myself a very modest lover
1355   and with one sole kiss satisfied,
                even if I long for many other things!
                [to Filli] Assured by your sweet words, divine and welcome,
                I will set you free,
                light of my eyes, and as assurance
1360   of what you have told me, a kiss I beg
                from your rosy and beautiful mouth.
                And if your kindness grants
                that I may at last link my spirit
                with these roses, where it lodges always,
1365   it would be much more agreeable to me than
                celestial nectar!

Filli   This is certainly a great demand!
                But the greater its value, the better you will be able
                to understand the desire that I have
1370   to serve you.

Satiro   I know well that it is a great demand
                and surely a faithful lover
                can have no more worthy gift
                from his dear nymph
                than a sweet kiss!

1375   It is so delightful
    that the soul, desiring a sweet death,
    comes to encounter itself
    with sweet kisses and acquires double life
    while kissed it kisses!

Filli   Therefore I am blessed, since such
    a good thing is granted to me! But you, my heart,
    must grant me only this, that I may tie
    your arms, so that you, from the sweetness
    that you will experience kissing me,
1385   won't embrace me so tightly
    that against your will
    I of you and you of me would remain deprived.

Satiro   You have tied my heart and you may now
    bind my arms! I am satisfied.

Filli   Then put your arms behind your back. O fortunate cord,
    since it is your destiny
    to tie such robust and beautiful arms!
    And you, leafy tree,
    well you may call yourself happy,
1395   since you hold fast the one who keeps
    my soul tied in so beautiful a knot.

Satiro   Don't tie me so tightly!

Filli   Calm down,
    and suffer for a moment:
    because the more tightly
1400   I tie you, the more safely
    I will then kiss you.

Satiro   Come on, do it quickly!

Filli   There, I have finished!

Satiro   Then, Filli,
    don't postpone my happiness
    and yours any longer!
1405   Since you have tied me so tightly
    that I won't be able to untie myself with a shake,

> grant me that blessing for which I so long
> that I cry like a bound lamb,
> only awaiting the desired end!

Filli   Certainly, I can make you wait no longer,
> nor do I want to wait to embrace you and sweetly
> kiss your delicate lips,
> which, if I understand aright,
> surpass the sweetness of Hyblean honey!

Satiro   Now what will you say
> when you have tried it?

Filli   Alas, I must consider!

Satiro   Come on then!

Filli   Will you resent it?
> Will you feel disgust for me? Tell me, my dear one.

Satiro   You would have me say something crazy!
1420   Now, how can I be disgusted by you
> when as much as life itself
> I love you and hold you dear?

Filli   You know that fear
> is natural in lovers, and I wouldn't want,
> instead of acquiring
1425   your good will, to deprive myself of it forever.

Satiro   Ah, don't be afraid of that
> which you mustn't fear.

Filli   For this I rejoice! But, my heart,
> you are so tall that I cannot reach
1430   this desired blessing! So, I must
> grab your beautiful beard
> with both hands
> like this: Bow your head!

Satiro   Oh me! Do it gently! What are you thinking?
1435   You are tearing off my beard! Stop, stop!

Filli	All right, I'll stop, but you mustn't move, so that I can give you a thousand kisses! O my horns, you have wounded my heart!
Satiro 1440	Oh me! Don't pull so hard! Don't twist my neck! Oh me, truly, you are hurting me!
Filli	Pardon me, my heart, I didn't mean to hurt you. Oh what soft breasts!
Satiro	Don't pinch so hard! Hey, stop it!
Filli 1445	Alas, I can't resist caressing you!
Satiro	Some beautiful caresses!
Filli	Oh, don't get angry, my dear life!
Satiro 1450	Let's kiss quickly, so we can make peace! If you don't kiss me, I will make your life miserable, and I will find myself another amorous nymph!
Filli	Shut your mouth! Do you want me to die of pain?
Satiro	Don't treat me so harshly! Now, what insanity is this that you continue to hurt me?
Filli	Ah, discourteous one, tell me, how is it that everything I do offends you? And yet, heaven is my witness, that all of it comes from too much love!
Satiro	[aside] Yes, I tell you, I have her whipped!
Filli	[aside] Oh, what an idiot!
Satiro	[aside] She weeps aside, as best I can tell.
Filli	[aside] I want to appear afflicted.

1460   [to Satiro] Oh me, what sorrow!
        This is what I am reduced to: my idol
        scorns me because I caress him too much!
        What should I do now? What can I do?

Satiro [aside] If I don't help this wretched girl,
1465   she is certain to end her life from grief!
        [to Filli] Filli, don't mourn! Let's make peace,
        and as a sign of our agreement, come at last,
        to kiss your beloved and your life:
        don't cry any more, for you alone will be
1470   my darling. Come, then, and give me a kiss.

Filli   Alas, my heart is encouraged
        by the sweet harmony of your words!
        And since you reinstate me
        in your favor, and desire
1475   that I kiss your dear and sweet mouth,
        I want first to eat
        a little bit of thyme, and I also want
        you to be so kind as to eat a small twig,
        so that our breath
1480   will be more delicate.
        Come now, I take it, and I am the first
        to try it. You take the rest.

Satiro Give it to me; I am content.

Filli   What do you think of it?

Satiro Oh me! what is this thing
1485   so bitter? I fear that you mock me
        and are making a fool of me! What kind of thyme
        is this you have given me?

Filli   O foolish one,
        now you finally understand
        that I have been mocking you! What woman,
1490   even if deformed and vile, could take pleasure
        in loving so monstrous and horrid a countenance?
        Now you see that I have caught you! Remain here,
        mocked, as you deserve to be, while I leave you.
        Would to heaven that you were prey

1495   of rabid bears and hungry wolves
so that I would never again encounter
your ugly face, which to me is the most
annoying and odious!

Satiro   Filli, Filli, where are you going? Stop, listen,
1500   at least untie me so that I do not become
a joke, a tale, and a game
for other pitiless nymphs like you!
Oh me, what can't a woman do
when she is resolved to deceive?
1505   With what flattery, oh me, with what words
she has convinced me,
to have my arms tied, as
she has already tied my heart and soul
with her long, flowing hair!

SCENE THREE

Gorgo the goatherd and Satiro

Gorgo   Damon, watch the flock
while I go to the hut to get some bread,
some cheese, some pears, and still other things
to make life serene, since I have
no other delight than eating.
1515   These lovers would have me believe
that nothing in the world is more delicious
nor gives greater contentment than love
when one is loved in return, and every day
they deafen my brain as they keep saying
1520   that nature should grant me no other
sense than taste,
because I am given only
to eating and drinking.
[They say] that [the sense] of sight is given to us,
1525   not only to see the lofty beauty
of heaven and earth,
but also to see
the great beauty of her whom one loves,
and to make her see
1530   with open eyes one's heart.

They say that the sense of hearing
is the reason that one hears
the sweet harmony
of the beloved siren,
1535   and because of this they have no envy
of the celestial harmony.
They also desire that one's sense of smell serve
not only for enjoying the various spring
flowers, but also for enjoying
1540   the sweet and delicate scents
that waft from the breast and golden hair
of their nymphs, and they believe that nature gave us
the sense of touch for enjoying the soft
and delicate breast of a beautiful woman,
1545   by whom one may support human offspring
in the world. They don't notice that I
make better use than they of these treasures
that courteous nature and heaven have given me,
nor like them do I ever curse them!
1550   For it often happens
that a lover becomes angry with his beloved,
and when he does, he curses his eyes and weeps
because nature has not made him blind,
for if he had not seen the beauty
1555   of his nymph, he would not have loved her.
If with haughty words she drives him away,
he would rather be deaf, and curses
because he wasn't born so, and if he cannot
smell that delicate breeze that he
1560   says wafts through her golden hair,
he would prefer not have such a sense at all,
rather than being deprived of the longed-for scent.
If he cannot enjoy her sweet kisses
and hold her hand,
1565   taste and touch he abhors equally.
And raving often,
they see the good, yet they long for evil!
However, these eyes are the reason that I rejoice
whenever I see a great abundance of food,
1570   and my sense of hearing comforts me whenever
I hear talk of filling one's stomach.
Of the sense of smell, I cannot tell you! Every time
I smell the precious odor

of smoking roast,
1575   I go wild over its sweetness!
Touch makes me feel
the height of delight whenever I
pet the fat sheep and calves, and I say,
"These will be good for my appetite!"
1580   But what will I say of taste? Alas, I cannot
express it in words, so great is the joy
that I feel when I think only of the great pleasure
that I find in drinking and eating!
Thus without reason these simple lovers
1585   reprove me, since I lavish
with such praise and useful exercise
all the gifts that Nature has given me.
Thus, she herself (she is so wise!) must
be obliged to me, since I strive
1590   to keep myself alive
with eating and drinking, while these lovers —
if they are loved — wear themselves out with
chasing their nymphs and serving them always.
Or, if they are not loved, for sorrow
1595   they kill themselves! Thus they are enemies
of themselves and also of nature,
for she didn't give them life just
so that they might kill themselves in various fashions!
But since I have better judgment than they do,
1600   I go happily to my hut
to fill this knapsack with food
and this jar with the liquor of Bacchus:
Sweet liquor, for which my heart always
lives, jubilant and happy, my blood sparkles,
1605   my eyes brighten, and my cheeks
flush, and so all the forces of the human body
are redoubled! Now, whoever wants
may follow Amore, but for as me, I will follow Ceres,
Bacchus, and their sweet fruits![4]

---

[4] Ceres was the daughter of Vesta and Saturn; she was the goddess of grains. Bacchus was the god of wine. This passage alludes to the proverb from Terence, "Sine Cerere et Libero friget Amor" (*Eunuchus*, line 732). It is alluded to again below in Gorgo's speech, lines 3191–3193. See the discussion of Andreini's incorporation of this proverb in the Introduction, xiv.

Satiro	Courteous farmer, let a storm
	not spoil your beautiful fields, so that you may
	gather in time the desired harvest!
	Grant to me, a sorrowful demigod,
	some merciful help!

Gorgo	Oh, poor thing!
1615	What terrible mistake
	has brought you here?

Satiro	Cruel Amore
	and the falsity of a nymph! Thus I swear to you
	by the Stygian wave[5] that in the future
	not only will I not desire to love any more nymphs,
1620	but I will also despise all of them and hold in contempt
	that traitor Amore who has led me
	with horrible pain into this condition, as you see!
	Untie me, I beg you,
	kind farmer, because my arms,
1625	which hurt me so, will soon be in agony!

Gorgo	You see that Gorgo has come here just in time?
	I will untie your arms, and I pray
	heaven that it will thus release you from the ties
	of that wicked boy, from whom derives
1630	all that is unhappy in this world!

Satiro	You may well believe that I will never again
	follow him who the world calls Amore,
	for his sweetness is none other than bitterness!

Gorgo	And I vow anew to myself
1635	never again to desire to follow any other
	pleasures than those of Bacchus and Ceres!

Satiro	Let's flee, flee Amore
	and also his mother,
	for they are the root of every evil!

---

[5] The "onda stigia," or "Stygian wave," refers to the river Styx, the river of the Underworld, or Hades. Arcadians took oaths by the river, swearing by the harmful properties of its waters. In Book Fourteen of the *Iliad*, Sleep makes Hera swear by the water of the Styx that she will give him Pasithea for his wife.

Gorgo	We will follow, follow Bacchus,[6]
	and Ceres and Pomona,[7]
	since for them in feast, game, and song
	everyone lives, cheerful and rejoicing!

Satiro	Let's go, for I want to give you in recompense
1645	for untying me
	a huge bearskin, that the day before yesterday
	a savage man gave me, along with the horns
	of a deer that he had
	killed by his own hand.

Gorgo	I thank you
1650	for this gift: if such things were
	fit to satisfy me,
	perhaps I would accept it.
	However, if you want to come
	to my hut, I will give you something other
1655	than the skin of a bear or branchy horns.

Satiro	Gorgo, if you don't want
	to accept this gift, at least accept
	my good intention, because I cannot
	give you anything else!

Gorgo	Come on, no more words!
1660	If you want to come with me, let's go, for I
	am dying of hunger! I feel my body lamenting
	and hear my guts making a loud noise because
	I have failed to give them the usual tribute,
1665	so I want to leave here!

Satiro	Let's go! I am also resolved to leave
	here, and I vow never to return
	to a place where I suffered anguish and scorn!
	[Now,] I will follow my companion Bacchus,
	Bacchus, lord and god of happiness!

---

[6] Andreini writes "Lieo," another name for Bacchus.

[7] Pomona was a nymph at Rome who guarded the fruit trees and gardens. She was worshipped as a goddess, and sacrifices were made to her in order to preserve the fruit crops.

Gorgo   Then let's go!

Satiro   We go, brother, we go!

SCENE FOUR

Filli and Mirtilla, nymphs

Filli   Certainly, Mirtilla, I would have rather believed
                 that the sun was deprived of light,
                 than that you were opposed to my pleasure,
                 and that you wanted to deprive me of that mercy
1675   won by my service and my love.

Mirtilla   Filli, that mercy of which you speak
                 is no more yours than mine!
                 I love Uranio, you know it, and I don't deny it,
                 and you love him and don't deny it, so we are forced
1680   to have between us sharp discord and war.

Filli   Amore was never pleased with company,
                 as you well know, Mirtilla!
                 So one of us must yield to the other.

Mirtilla   Come now, no more argument!
1685   Don't you remember, Filli, that we have spoken
                 of our quarrel
                 with Opico, among all others the most learned,
                 to whose wise counsel
                 we have submitted each of our disputes?
1690   And he desires that the singing of
                 one of us settle this complaint between us.

Filli   I have not forgotten
                 what he recommended to us, and I marvel
                 that he delays so long
1695   to come to us with his instrument[8]
                 that he plays with such a skilled hand.
                 Now if heaven is willing, when we have

---

[8] In lines 1728-1729, the instrument is said to be of "hollowed wood," so it is a wind instrument, a pipe or flute.

attuned our singing to his music,
he will bring accord to
1700   our amorous dispute.

Mirtilla   He has sent us here and cannot delay
             much longer. Ah, here he is!

SCENE FIVE

Opico, shepherd, Filli and Mirtilla, nymphs

Opico   Heaven preserve you, gentle and worthy
             pair, whose beauty
1705   adorns these woods and this age
             like the stars the heaven, and the flowers the hillside!

Filli   Opico, welcome!

Mirtilla   If you had delayed much longer,
             a harsh quarrel would have broken out anew between us!

Opico   Pardon me, nymphs, for Selvaggio[9]
             held me at bay for a long time.
             But now let me stand between you
             amorous nymphs.

Filli   Stand here.

Opico   Thus I am rejuvenated! O beautiful nymphs,
1715   how much I envy the one for whom you languish!
             If I were like him, young and handsome,
             I would rather die
             than ever make you suffer.
             But it is time to carry out
1720   what we have planned.
             Come now! Sing your songs along with the music,
             for we are in a very beautiful place in the shade,

---

[9] "Selvaggio" means savage or wild man. Selvaggio, "a wild man," appears in the scenario *Il Mago*, or *The Magician*: see Lea, *Italian Popular Comedy*, 610–15. Selvaggio is also the name of a shepherd from the scenario *Proteo*, or *Proteus*, and the character's name appears in *Il Pantaloncino*, or *Pantaloonlet*: see Lea, *Italian Popular Comedy*, 621–42.

where Flora reposes among the flowers
in the embrace of her husband,[10]
1725   and he for her sweetness
wafts gentle breezes through these leafy branches,
and the murmur of the waves
will provide the sound
of the hollowed wood.[11]
1730   Now you begin, Filli,
and then you follow, Mirtilla.
Sing, then, in a contest,
for the Muses love singing in turn.

Filli   Learned Calliope,
1735   mother of that good Thracian,[12]
who attracted to himself the most fierce and swift animals
with his sonorous voice,
inspire, O goddess, in this voice of mine
sweet melody!

Mirtilla   O father of the Muses,[13]
come today into my song and into my heart,
into my heart that grows weak
from your studies no less than from the torch
of my enemy Amore!
1745   May Peneus's scornful daughter wear
her first beautiful limbs
in order to take pity on you.[14]

---

[10] Flora, the goddess of flowers and gardens for the Romans, was married to Zephyr, one of the winds. It is said that he gave her the right to preside over the flowers and perpetual youth. Through his sweet breath, Zephyr was able to produce flowers and fruits.

[11] The hollowed wood is his pipe or flute; the reference is to air moving through it to make it sound.

[12] Calliope, one of the muses, was the daughter of Jupitor and Mnemosyne. Her son Orpheus (fathered by either Apollo or Oeger, depending on the story), played his lyre so well that rivers would stop running, mountains would move, and wild beasts would draw near to hear his playing. It is also noteworthy that Calliope was credited with settling the dispute between Prosperpine and Venus over Adonis.

[13] Jupiter, or Jove, as Andreini calls him, was the father of the muses. With Mnemosyne, he had nine daughters who were the goddesses of music, poetry, dancing, and all the liberal arts. They were Clio, Euterpe, Thalia, Melpomene, Terpsichore, Erato, Polyhymnia, Calliope, and Urania.

[14] Daphne was the daughter of the river Peneus. Her mother was the goddess Terra. Apollo pursued Daphne, but with the aid of the gods she was changed into a laurel.

Filli	Four and six apples gathered from a single branch
	I keep in my hut, and I promise them
1750	to my charming shepherd whom I love so much!

Mirtilla	A sling from me with beautiful work
	made of fine silk and decorated in gold
	will be a gift for him whom I love and adore!

Filli	How many sighs and lamentations will I give forth
1755	before my most cruel shepherd
	at last shows pity for my suffering?

Mirtilla	Who doesn't know how many times I have made
	these hills tepid and soaked with my tears,
	to vent my sorrowful pain?

Filli	Igilio gave me two young doves
	day before yesterday, and Clori almost
	died for envy, so charming and beautiful they were!

Mirtilla	Two baskets of flowers Alcon gave to me,
	and Amaranta, already mad from wrath,
1765	turned her feet elsewhere, so as not to see them!

Filli	What does filling heaven with cries avail, alas,
	or causing the waters to rise with my weeping,
	if it doesn't earn belief in my great suffering?

Mirtilla	I love cruel Uranio and do not regret it,
1770	for his beauty, which pleases all eyes,
	makes me happy to rejoice in every torment!

Filli	The snow melts in the sun, and the fire
	melts the wax, and, as for me, the disdain and anger
	of Uranio consume my heart little by little.

Mirtilla	The sheep benefit from grass, as do the bees from flowers,
	but the only thing that benefits me is to contemplate
	the beautiful face and vivid coloring of Uranio!

Filli	Tell me, nymph, what is the animal
	that is formed in water, then lives in flame,
1780	and this golden arrow will be yours!

Mirtilla	Tell me which fish hides in the ocean and makes whoever barely touches it tremble, and you will have two white and fertile kids!
Opico 1785	No more, amorous nymphs! I am ready to end this amorous dispute of yours: There is no contest between you, where there is such a great likeness in valor! I swear to you by the other gods that in my opinion you are equals in beauty and in singing! However, I must say that you toil in vain, for each of you follows and loves Uranio, yet you must have noticed by now that he loves only Ardelia and cares only for Ardelia. So, put away the discord between you, O daughters, and abandon loving one who does not love you!

Lines 1790, 1795 appear in left margin.

Filli	This seems impossible to me, for I am not powerful enough to do that which Amore does not desire!
Mirtilla	While I have a spirit and a soul, I will love only Uranio!
Opico 1805	I do not wish to oppose your desires, but since you cannot or do not want to stop loving him who does not love you, at least for the sake of my love, let there be no argument between you, and endeavor, united in virtue and beautiful works, to acquire both his love and his good will.
Filli 1815	Moved by your valid reasons, I am happy to obey you, and I promise you to love Mirtilla the same as myself! And I pray that heaven will allow me (if I am deemed worthy of it) to possess the heart of Uranio. If heaven still denies me this, [I pray that] the love of Igilio move and transform my heart, so that Igilio may enter where first there was Uranio.

Mirtilla	And I vow to you, my Opico, to have
	toward gentle Filli the same
1820	friendly intention that she promises
	so sweetly to have for me, and here
	I join my hand with hers
	as a pledge of my faith. I also pray
	that the stars either grant me my beloved
1825	(if I am deemed worthy of it) or at least not deny me
	the pleasure of my former freedom.

Opico	So just are your demands
	that you can be assured
	that you will undoubtedly obtain them. But it is time
1830	that I go to Dameta, who, having need
	of my advice,
	awaits me at the spring. Remain in peace!

| Filli | Opico, I thank you! |

| Mirtilla | And I thank you, too, my Opico! |

| Filli | It's also time for us to go. |

The End of Act Three

ACT FOUR
SCENE ONE

Opico and Tirsi, shepherds

Opico	Now, Tirsi, have you noticed
	the tearful state
	of unhappy Uranio?
	He leans against that dry and withered tree trunk,
1840	with his languid eyes fixed
	unmoving on the ground,
	so immersed in his sorrow
	that not only has he not seen us,
	but he hasn't heard us, either,
1845	even though we have greeted him
	in a most loud and friendly way!
Tirsi	I have unfortunately understood
	that unhappy Uranio is as dejected as
	a turtledove who has lost his mate!
1850	But if Uranio felt even once
	the thousandth part of the pleasures
	that are experienced in the hunt,
	they would put out of his mind
	the pain he suffers,
1855	and he would no longer continue to follow in vain
	the pitiless Ardelia, for whom I fear
	that one day he will cut short his life.
Opico	I vow to you, Tirsi, by this hair of mine
	already made squalid and white,
1860	as you see, by the hand of time,
	that when I saw him (alas) being this way,
	pensive and mute, it took great effort to hold back

my tears; and although
my passionate flames are all spent,
1865   it reminded me of my own past anguish
in my greener and more flowering years.
But if Uranio has not yet tried
the pleasures of the hunt
[aside] (and only this exercise
1870   could, if the truth I discern,
perhaps banish his amorous fire,
because removing idleness also gets rid of
all the force with which Amore attacks us!)
it does not astonish me, for I am
1875   already old, and anyway
I never felt such pleasures.
But tell me, dear Tirsi,
why do you have such great relish for the hunt?

Tirsi   Opico, it is easy to see
1880   that you have never experienced such a pleasure,
for if you had, you would never ask
such a question of me!
But you must understand that there is no delight in the world
that can equal that of the hunt,
1885   or the immense pleasure
that I experience, when in a small boat
with a companion or two I go happily about,
disturbing the fish and the marsh birds
of their sweet repose,
1890   with the bait, the fishhooks, and the net.
We never return
to our huts
unless the little boat is all loaded
with beautiful and rich prey. And if I wanted
1895   to describe to you the beautiful ways
with which we are occupied, I know for certain
that, even though you are old, you would not give up
this sweet pleasure
for any other!

Opico   Indeed, I regard it as
a pleasant thing,
but doesn't it ever bore you, Tirsi,
and make you feel you've had enough?

	There is no pleasure in the world so great
1905	that it doesn't finally become too much.

Tirsi   When this
pleasure bores me, at once I take
other nets and go with the same
companions into some solitary valley.
There among the thick, leafy branches
1910   we spread our net,
so thin that the eye can barely see it;
then with clods, stones,
and cries we put the birds in flight!
They, simple little ones, rise in vain,
1915   in fearful flight, trying to get away,
but they fly into the trap,
and to our satisfaction they remain prisoners.
Afterwards, when we see that the net
is so loaded that it can barely hold them,
1920   little by little we loosen
the ends of the rope, and inside
we find diverse birds in such abundance
that we don't know where to put them, and often
we carry to our lodgings
1925   the net with the birds
still caught in it.

Opico   It is unfortunately true
that he who fears misfortune more than he should,
instead of fleeing it, sometimes
1930   stumbles right into the worst of it! The birds
of which you speak bear witness: they,
fearing a slight noise, flee it, and
run inadvertently to their deaths.
But continue, if you please, for it seems
1935   I have before me all that you are
so skillfully describing.

Tirsi   Now listen, my Opico, to the manner in which
we enjoy this sweet sport and in how many ways
we make diverse prey of different birds.
1940   Far away from my hut,
as far as one would shoot an arrow six times,
sits a shady valley

of such beauty that it doesn't envy even that of
the famous Ida,
1945   where the three goddesses were judged.[1]
This one is surrounded by
beautiful views and gently rolling hills,
among which one higher than the others
can be seen. And above this
1950   [is] a charming little forest
of laurels that are always green and
sweet-scented junipers and myrtles.
There we have built
a little hut, and from every tree around it
1955   we have cut the branches,
so that when eager birds swoop down,
looking for a place put their feet,
they place them on the viscous twig traps
that we have arranged between the trees
1960   for stopping them in flight.
Then we, silent and hidden
in the little lodging
made of supple reeds,
with deceptive song
1965   imitate the voice
of the thrushes that, passing by,
allow themselves to be tricked by the feigned sound.
Flying [ever] more slowly,
they circle around until they fall to their deaths.
1970   Then, to the other thrushes
that we keep alive in a cage for such a use,
we show the screech-owl, and, as soon as
they see it, they raise their voices
as they usually do — either for fear
1975   or else for hate: I can affirm
neither the one nor the other for you.
But it is enough, however, that the wandering thrushes
run with quick and frantic flight,
rashly, to their unforeseen ill.
1980   And you would certainly laugh [upon] seeing
how and how much they toil in vain,

---

[1] Andreini refers to Mount Ida, where the shepherd Paris judged the beauty contest
among Venus, Pallas, and Juno, awarding Venus the golden apple.

                striving to free themselves: while they try
                to untangle their feet, they entangle their wings!
                After that, everyone fills his knapsack with them.

Opico   Similar to these birds
                are rash lovers,
                who allow themselves to be enticed by the song
                and the sweetest words
                of their nymphs, and then
1990   in the unyielding birdlime traps,
                [because] of their cruel nature, they lose their life.
                But if among us there were
                some new Medea
                who rejuvenated me,[2] I promise you
1995   that I would like to spend some of my time
                in such sweet sports!

Tirsi   I won't speak, then, of other methods
                that we use to catch diverse kinds
                of birds, and I will only mention what pleasure
2000   one experiences in following
                the timid little deer, and the fearful hares,
                the soft rabbits, and the nimble goats,
                all of which I easily catch, some with dogs,
                others with darts, and still others with snares.
2005   But what shall I say of bringing down a bear
                or a fierce wild boar with the sharp spear?
                Certainly the sun could turn three times and four
                toward the east
                before I could tell you
2010   enough of the pleasure that I experience
                in the hunt, and I am sure, as long as
                there are birds in the air, fish in the water, and
                wild beasts in the forest, that by virtue of my nets,
                my hooks, my traps,
2015   my snares, my dogs, my arrows,

---

[2] See the Prologue, note 10. For Andreini's theme in this passage, Medea serves as an excellent symbol of the dangerous beloved who entraps the foolish lover. The choice of Medea is also important for the old shepherd Opico because Medea, with her skilled knowledge of herbs, filled the veins of Æson, the father of Jason, with the juices of certain herbs, and he was rejuvenated.

	and this bow that was given to me as a gift
	from the goddess of the first heaven,[3]
	I will never lack pleasures and sports!
	Because of this bow, Amore doesn't dare
2020	accost me at all,
	for he fears being wounded himself,
	instead of wounding me!

Opico   Don't say such things, son!
Don't be so bold, for excessive
boldness often leads some to death!
2025   Remember Icarus and Phaethon![4]
But, I can no longer stay here with you;
therefore, I leave you to god, gentle Tirsi.

Tirsi   Farewell, Opico! [to himself] This old man believes
that by disparaging Amore, I do an outrage
2030   to some god, but I am not so bold,
nor so foolhardy
that I scorn the gods. I honor and venerate them,
but not him, who is no god! But whom do I see
coming toward me so happily?
2035   This is good Coridone, who, in addition to his custom
of knowing the woods, perceives
the great secrets of the spacious sky. And even though he is
a citizen of the forests, he is
nevertheless given to these beneficial studies,
2040   of the tilling of the soil as well
as of everything that best suits man!

---

[3] The "goddess of the first heaven" is Diana, goddess of the hunt. The "first heaven" began just beyond the moon's orbit.

[4] Icarus was the son of Dedalus, who fled Crete with wings held together by wax. He foolishly flew too high, the sun melted his wings, and he fell into the Aegean sea. Phaethon was a handsome and rash young man of whom Venus became enamored. She gave him the care of one of her temples, and this favor made him even more vain and bold. He sought out Phoebus (another name for Apollo) and demanded to be allowed to drive his chariot, or the sun, across the sky as proof that Phoebus was his true father. Phoebus acquiesced; the chariot's horses, however, rebelled, and when Jupiter perceived that earth was in danger of being hit by the sun, he hurled a lightning bolt at the driver, striking him down. Phaethon burned to death as he fell into the Po.

Scene Two

Coridone and Tirsi, shepherds

Coridone   God save you, good Tirsi!

Tirsi   O Coridone, welcome!
             Where are you going?

Coridone   It is has been quite a while
2045   since I left my hut
             to look for my beautiful Nisa.
             Nisa is as loved by Coridone,
             as Coridone is loved by Nisa!

Tirsi   Tell me, who has so much delayed you?

Coridone   Only you!

Tirsi   And why do you come to me now?

Coridone   Know that near here I saw
             wise Opico, who stood with you,
             so I came closer and listened as
             you reasoned with him. Since
2055   I know for a fact that he is never in the habit
             of listening to something that is not worthy
             to be heard, I became
             desirous to hear [such] a notable thing. I slowed
             my long steps, leaned upon a flowering ash,
2060   and listened attentively to what was said.
             I know and confess truly
             that the sports of the hunt
             are pleasing and sweet, but in respect
             to the pleasures of love,
2065   they are shadow, smoke, dream, mist, and wind!

Tirsi   If everyone in that fellow's kingdom[5]
             is as happy as Uranio, and if the pleasures

---

[5] The kingdom is Amore's.

that [Amore] grants you are like his,
everyone among you should be sorry that he is liberal
2070   with his gifts to you! Everyone should strive
to make him a miser! O miserable lovers,
for a lying look, for a
perfidious and inconstant eyebrow,
for a feigned smile,
2075   and for a sweet but traitorous word,
to lose in an instant
the dear liberty, the free will, the heart,
to make of one's own desires
a cruel tyrant!
2080   Wily, flattering, and false nymph!
O blind minds, O vain and crazy thoughts!

Coridone   Please forgive, Amore, this fellow who is not familiar with
the gifts of your reign!
He must not be aware that highest Jove
2085   descended to earth to enjoy your graces
as a bellowing bull, a burning flame, and a singing swan,
as well as a rapacious eagle, a rain of gold,
and a leaping satyr: in short,
he hid himself in diverse forms,
2090   little caring about jealous Juno,
in order to taste your joys and delights.
Tirsi, I do confess that he who is a follower and servant
of Amore sustains some annoyance,
but the pains of love are so sweet
2095   that even while tormenting, they offer comfort,
and a little sweetness appeases much bitterness!

Tirsi   I will never believe that sweet fruit
comes from bitter seed.

Coridone   If you didn't mind listening to me,
2100   perhaps I would make you repent of this.[6]

---

[6] Andreini writes, "forse ti renderei di ciò pentito," in which case "pentito" comes
from "pentirsi" and may also mean to change one's mind. Next, however, there is the play
on words that encompasses both "to change one's mind" and "to repent," as the following
lines show.

Tirsi	Only one who errs repents: I have not committed
	any error, and thus in vain you attempt
	to make me repent! But I wish to please you.
	Come on, then, recount at last these sweetnesses,
2105	so full of wormwood and gall!

Coridone	Do you think, Tirsi, that to have in abundance
	a woolly flock and to be rich
	in all seasons with fresh milk,
	to have flowered pastures
2110	and a flourishing herd,
	fertile hillsides and thick leafy woods,
	charming hills and plentiful springs,
	dogs and servants, and all those things, in short,
	that make a shepherd joyful and merry,
2115	are for their owner a great satisfaction?

Tirsi	Not only do I think it, but I believe it,
	for riches bring quiet to the
	soul and heart, without which
	one can never know what thing is good.

Coridone	And do you think that happy is the gentle soul
	to have the Muses as friends,
	to know how with sweet and learned skill
	to give breath to the waxed uneven reeds,
	to sing to the music of sylvan oats
2125	sweet verses and to teach them to the stones,
	where Echo remains buried,
	who never grows tired of repeating
	final accents?[7] Do you think that it is
	of great satisfaction to know how to prune
2130	the dry and barren branches with the scythe,
	to know when and how
	one must make the grafts;
	when to marry the vines to the elms;[8]

---

[7] After being rejected by Narcissus, Echo hid among the caves and cliffs until her bones turned to stone, and nothing was left of her but her voice.

[8] Andreini writes, "quando le viti maritar agli olmi." One could also translate it, "when to unite the vines with the elms." This "marriage" image is an old one in pastoral poetry, going back to Virgil, *Georgics* 1.2–3. Andreini's lines echo the opening passage of the *Georgics*:

when to strip the leaves from the plants,
2135   to shear the flock; and when
to press the swollen udders and extract from them
the sweet milk, then make cheese from it;
and how to rend the earth with the plow,
and when is the right time to draw the honey
2140   from the bees; when the grapes
must be gathered and their liquor squeezed from them?
Do you believe, Tirsi, that it is of great satisfaction
to know how to heal the flock
when from the hoar-frost
2145   they contract scabies or gout,
and to know how to guard them against a charm?
And to know how with the scythe
to cut from the green meadows
the grassy fruit, or from the beloved fields
2150   to pull up the useless bracken, couch-grass
and the wretched tare, that to the blond
spikes of wheat is so harmful? And then when
to cut down the corn with a smaller scythe?
Oh, tell me, Tirsi, is it not a great satisfaction
2155   to understand fully the course of the stars,
the power of the planets, and why the sun
sets in the bosom of Tethys;[9]
why the moon changes;
why the earth often
2160   intervenes between the sun and his sister;
why the days are short and why they are long,
according to when the sun stays away or draws near;
why from the third heaven sweetness rains down;
why lazy Saturn is full of venom,
2165   and Mars is full of arrogance and ire?
Why Jove is benign; and why the year
has so many and such varied seasons?

What makes the crops joyous, beneath what star, Maecenas, it is well to turn the
soil, and wed vines to elms, what tending the cattle need, what care the herd in
breeding, what skill the thrifty bees — hence shall I begin my song." (1.1-5)

See also Virgil's *Eclogues* 2.76 for a sarcastic use of the vines and elms image. The image
appears again below in lines 2239-2241.

    [9] Tethys, a great sea goddess, was the wife of Oceanus, and the daughter of Uranus and
Terra. She was the mother of the great rivers of the earth, and her name is frequently used
poetically to mean the sea itself.

	And finally, is it not a great satisfaction
	to know how to investigate the deep secrets
2170	of nature and heaven? And [to know] that there's nothing
	that hides from our intellect?

Tirsi   Certainly, yes, Coridon, for our knowledge
           distinguishes us from animals,[10]
           and because of our intelligence we come
2175   almost as equals to highest Jove.

Coridone   Oh, Tirsi, even though riches and wisdom
           are considered gifts of great value, they are nothing like
           the delights of love,
           which have no equal!
2180   Have you not heard old Melibeo say
           that the Phrygian shepherd[11]
           refused to give the golden apple to Pallas,[12]
           so wise, or to Queen Juno,[13]
           only to give it to amorous Venus?
2185   Wise he [Paris] was to prize the embraces
           and the amorous joys of a beautiful woman,
           more than profound knowledge, more than riches!

Tirsi   Until now, I have believed that the hunt
           was, of every pleasure, the pleasure most sweet;
2190   and if I heard someone discussing
           other delights, I fled him, little
           esteeming his wisdom. This is the reason
           that I did not pay attention
           to the sage reasoning of Melibeo!
2195   Finally, until now I believed

---

[10] In lines 2172–2175, Andreini has Tirsi say, "Certo sì, Coridon, poiché dai bruti / ci distingue il sapere; / e per la conoscenza al sommo Giove / quasi veniamo eguali," which echoes lines from Dante's *Inferno* (26: 119–120): "fatti non foste a viver come bruti, / ma per seguir virtute e conoscenza" — "You were not born to live like brutes / but to pursue virtue and knowledge!" The translation of Dante's lines is by Charles S. Singleton.

[11] Paris was the shepherd elected to give the prize to the most beautiful of the three goddesses.

[12] Pallas, also known as Athena and Minerva, to note only three of her several names, was the goddess of wisdom. She had no mother, but sprang forth directly from Jupiter's brain.

[13] Juno was the daughter of Saturn and Ops, and she was both sister and wife to Jupiter. Her marriage to Jupiter made her the queen of all the gods, as well as of heaven and earth.

that love was the plague of mortals,
and did not believe that there was any joy
in either the face or the bosom of a beautiful nymph,
but your speech is so sweet and gentle
2200   that my obstinate heart is somewhat softened.

Coridone   Tirsi, so much sweetness love has placed
in the charming nymphs, that one
may call himself three times blessed,
if he becomes the lover of one of them!
2205   And you can believe that those who are called
to so great a good do not envy Jove
his celestial throne.
Amore never brings
any harm to mortals!
2210   Amore is the life of the world and the true guardian
of the living; he preserves and rules
over all human affairs, and his celestial
torch encourages all! And know, Tirsi,
that because of him alone is the woman so dear
2215   to the man, and whoever flees her, also flees
from the most worthy and noble part of himself.

Tirsi   And therefore, a man cannot survive in the world
without a woman?

Coridone   Just as a man
may live without her, so she may
2220   sustain her fragile life without a man.
Thus, so sweet and dear
is this heaven-given companionship,
and so sweet is marital passion,
that it sustains them together,
2225   but one deprived of the other
either doesn't live or lives poorly.
What more? The plants themselves perceive
the great power of Amore!
But because love does not grow
2230   without its prized companion,
all the plants that are without the male
or else without the female, are slow.
The ivy and the cypress show this clearly,
and the almond alone produces little fruit.

2235	The palm without its male doesn't reproduce,
	but if they are near each other, one bends
	with natural love toward his dear,
	sweet companion,
	and they compete to make fruit. The twisted
2240	vines gladly embrace the elm
	and the poplar [as] their dear husbands; the myrtle
	loves the white olive.
	The birds also love each other — the male dove
	loves his dear female dove, and the others do likewise.
2245	In short the sea, the earth and heaven are full
	of love. There was never an age, there was never a sex
	that survived without love!
	Every animal, both with reason and without,
	boldly scorns every peril
2250	to enjoy the sweetness of love,
	and doesn't turn down manifest death.
	Love, therefore, you also! Experience how much
	happiness there is in loving a nymph that loves you!
	Go with her about these valleys,
2255	gathering flowers and weaving garlands;
	and as many flowers as are interwoven in the garlands,
	that many kisses give to her,
	and from her that many you will have!
	Experience how great a joy it is to see
2260	a dainty hand adorn your temples
	with a beautiful little garland!
	Oh, try a little of the joy that there is
	in sitting in the shade of the flowered hills,
	singing of either the eyes or the golden hair
2265	of a beautiful nymph, and making the banks sound
	with her lovely name! Try how pleasant it is
	that she interrupts your words often
	with her dear and sweet kisses!
	Try, oh try, what joy is to be
2270	found in a grotto of pleasant cool shadows,
	while the sun with its burning rays scorches the earth,
	in the lap of a charming nymph,
	who, after a thousand amorous little jokes,
	sweet words, and gentle sighs,
2275	takes off your clothes so that the pleasant breeze
	with its coolness refreshes you,
	and sings sweet, amorous little verses

to entice you to sleep,
in the meantime shooing away the importunate fly.
2280   Then, drawing fresh flowers
from her white breast and her golden tresses,
she makes them into a crown for you,
and with a white veil,
while sweetly you sleep,
2285   she either strokes your forehead or fans the gentle breezes,
until, wide awake, together you go
to the fortunate inn,
to pass the happy nocturnal hours.
Then with the dawning day
2290   these sweet pleasures return anew!

Tirsi   Though it appears to me an incredible thing,
that what you recount
may be of such contentment, nevertheless
I feel some pleasure in listening to you,
2295   so, if [you have] more to say about this, continue!

Coridone   Believe, O my Tirsi, that there is no happiness
that can equal this delight,
this great sweetness, this joy
that lovers experience, when without
2300   suspicion and jealousy
they love each other. I will not speak of the joy
that in the beginning they experience while
their love grows into a beautiful flame.
I will not speak of that pleasure, however immense,
2305   that one feels drinking through the lights[14]
the soul of whom one loves. Furthermore, I will say
       nothing of
that delight that the ears send
to the heart upon hearing the clear and beloved voice.
I will leave aside the delightful meetings,
2310   the attractions, the favors, the charms, the gifts,
and much more than the gifts, the precious stolen [moments],
holding hands so sweetly,
and a thousand other contentments! I will speak only
of that sweet pleasure that has no equal,

---

[14] Andreini uses "le luci," or the lights, which refer to the eyes. See commentary on Andreini's Petrarchism in the Introduction, xvi.

2315   of that pleasure, when lovers and spouses,
     after some sighs and some drops
     of little tears, rest secure upon the grass and the flowers
     or in a dark cave,
     of the delights of love
2320   a faithful secretary,[15]
     and without fear, without holding back
     they show each other their open hearts,
     and reveal their thoughts, remembering
     past suffering. In the joy
2325   of the happy present, each grief is forgotten,
     and if from bitterness and anguish
     they wept in the past, now they each bathe their face
       and breast
     with tears for the sweetness
     of their loves. Oh, how delightful is that murmur
2330   they make with low voices,
     that sussurration of kisses either given or taken,
     that lingering look into the two beloved lights,
     enamored lights. One beloved
     mouth utters ardent sighs, and
2335   the other catches them.
     Oh, words, sighs, kisses, spirits
     hot, sweet, and gentle, beloved and dear,
     that emerge from those lips! O surpassing human
     sweetness, O inestimable pleasure,
2340   O goodness unrecognized and unappreciated
     if one never tries it! Oh, how miserable
     are the shepherds and nymphs
     who do not experience the great sweetness of love,
     who do not realize that youth
2345   was given to us by heaven and nature
     to be employed in their delightful games.
     Whoever allows his age to pass
     without the grace of love in April or May,
     in time sees his error, [and realizes] that it would be
2350   much better not to have such knowledge!
     Therefore there is no happiness in the world
     greater than that of two loving hearts
     whom marital love ties and unites.

---

[15] For secretary, Andreini uses "segretaria," meaning the keeper of their secrets.

Tirsi	Oh, say no more!
2355	What you have told me has so softened

my hard heart that I am no longer as I was:
On the contrary, I burn with desire to make myself
   the servant
of a charming nymph!

Coridone	Well, bless you four times and six,
2360	if you are ready to undertake such a commendable task!

But now I must leave to go in search of
my beautiful Nisa, who with her white foot
causes roses and lilies to bloom
wherever she goes![16]

2365   My charming and beautiful Nisa —
at the appearance of her beautiful ardent eyes
the torrents stop;
the valleys, hills, and meadows rejoice!
Nisa, whom not even the splendor of the sun

2370   can equal, and there is no flower whose beauty can
conquer hers! Farewell — remain in peace!

Tirsi   Go, happy and content!
It is surely true, yet I scarcely believe
how Coridone's shrewd speech

2375   has aroused my mind that until now
has been asleep! But what beauty
is this? What splendor dazzles my eyes?

SCENE THREE

Mirtilla and Tirsi

Mirtilla   Unhappy me, I don't know where
my destiny is guiding me! I deceive myself

2380   like an enchanted snake that agitates itself
in order not to not to go where
the magic draws it.
May it ever happen that if the cruel Uranio
knew how I live,

---

[16] Andreini writes, "col bianco piede / nascer fa gigli e rose," which may also be translated, "with her white foot / gives birth to lilies and roses."

2385	unhappy, or better to say,
	how I die for him,
	would he allow me to die? Alas, even if he saw it,
	he unfortunately wouldn't believe it!

Tirsi   [aside] I will try, if I'm in luck,
2390   to talk with her. [to Mirtilla] Heaven save you,
          beautiful nymph, splendor of these woods!

Mirtilla Welcome, shepherd, whoever you might be.

Tirsi   I am Tirsi, son of the learned Alcimedonte
          and Licori who have already
2395   gone on, happy ones, to a more tranquil life,
          leaving me heir to ample riches:
          all the flock that grazes on Aracynthus[17]
          is mine, with sheep so numerous,
          that the mortal eye cannot count them all,
2400   and close to Erymanthus[18] in a thousand meadows
          Alphesiboeus[19] nourishes and cares for
          my prosperous herd, so never
          do I lack fresh milk!
          And if it pleases you to know how
2405   agile I am, charming nymph, know
          that no shepherd so dexterous or quick as I am
          (nor do I speak of an unfamiliar thing) lives
          who is my equal in racing or wrestling,
          throwing the stake or hurling darts,
2410   wounding a savage beast with the bow
          or flinging heavy stones with the sling!
          I sing as Mopso[20] used to sing,
          whose name yet lives throughout the woods,
          and is esteemed among the nymphs and shepherds.
2415   That lyre, that my dear father
          left me, I play so sweetly

---

[17] Aracynthus is a mountain upon which Aphrodite/Venus had a temple; her surname of Aracynthias is derived from its name.

[18] Erymanthus is the name of a mountain, a river, and a town in Arcadia.

[19] Alphesiboeus is a shepherd mentioned in Virgil's *Eclogues*, in particular in *Eclogue* 8 in which his song is credited with magical powers.

[20] Andreini seems to relate her Mopso to Mopsus, a prophet or seer, much celebrated during the Trojan War. "Mopsus" is also a shepherd name frequently used in pastoral poetry. He is a character in Virgil's *Eclogue* 5 and is mentioned in *Eclogue* 8.

that the Napaeae and the Naiads[21] often leave
their seats and come joyfully toward the sound,
dancing with damp feet in a contest.
2420   Now do not scorn me, gentle nymph:
welcome this heart that for you alone
is already all full of amorous fire!
And if thundering Jove and the other gods
prize the first fruits of the shepherds,
2425   you must also prize, my mortal goddess,
the first fruits of my heart that I consecrate to you.

Mirtilla   I understand from what you say, gentle shepherd,
that you are a new follower of Amor;
therefore, you do not know that where Amore
2430   once strikes, for this wound
death is the only medicine. Now you should know that I
love and revere Uranio, who is as cruel
(O misery) as he is handsome, yet whoever would
draw his beautiful image from my breast,
2435   would also have to be able to draw the stars
from the sky, to take away the bright
light from the sun, and to illuminate the night!
Thus, Amor prevents me from accepting these first fruits
that you would like to give me —
2440   so leave Mirtilla and follow another!

Tirsi   Mirtilla, my soul, who deserve so much,
if Uranio does not prize your love,
give it to me, for to me it will be more dear
than this life!

Mirtilla   A true servant of Amore
cannot give her heart but to one!

Tirsi   I know — but if the gift is not welcomed by him
to whom it is given, doesn't the gift
of the giver become free again,
2450   as it was before?
And, if your gracious offering

---

[21] The Napææ were the deities who presided over hills and woods, while the Naiads were those who presided over springs, rivers, fountains, and wells.

is rejected, I nevertheless
will accept it gladly, O beautiful
and gracious nymph! And if you
2455   accept me as yours, you will see my flock
dancing and my horned herd
skipping for joy!

Mirtilla   If it were as you say with my gift,
then I would be able to render you
2460   the favor you ask of me, but you must know
that Uranio gladly accepted as a gift
my burning heart, not really to keep it
in his white breast, but to torture it
most cruelly! Yet, if he keeps it,
2465   it is truly just that to him alone
I turn and him alone I love! And even if I wanted
to love you, I could not love you from the heart,
for I am deprived of it.

Tirsi   Mirtilla, my death, I will not say life,
2470   could you bear that I languish
only to love you as much as my eyes?
Don't you know that it is a proverb spoken by
nature, love the one who loves you?

Mirtilla   Alas, if each beloved one loves returned love
2475   by natural custom, I would not be
as you see me, afflicted and malcontent!
Your suffering truly pains me, because I know for a fact
how unhappy and miserable is the lover
who is not requited!
2480   But know that no object
pleases my eyes but the charming Uranio —
Uranio is the only one who holds my soul,
and it desires no other shelter
or sweeter prison!
2485   And because every other sight is a nuisance to me,
I leave you and go in search of him.

Tirsi   Oh, who deprives me of admiring, alas,
her serene beauty? Who separates me
from my beautiful sun and takes her away and steals her?
2490   Alas, can I no longer gaze at her,

she who alone makes me happy and joyful?
Oh, how sharp and stinging
your departure is to me, my soul!
O fugitive nymph, at least wait
2495   so that I may worship you as a goddess, since
you refuse to be loved as a nymph.
Now with my pain I know and attest
how great is the force of love!
There is nothing on earth
2500   that does not yield to Amore!
But I will follow her because, with her departure,
she has taken with her my soul!

SCENE FOUR

Ardelia, nymph

The summer heat and the fleeing beast
have made me more flushed than usual;
2505   my hair, that at first was dry,
is now damp from perspiration,
and my lips are parched. It's a good idea
to refresh myself a bit in this spring.
But what do I see? At what do I look
2510   in the liquid crystal?
Charming nymph, indeed charming goddess,
may heaven, from whence I believe that you have descended,
always preserve your beauty!
I bow down to you
on my knees and in my heart,
2515   and I accept you as my goddess!
See how courteously she either responds
to my salute or seems to respond —
and she, like me, moves her lips
as I move my lips, and bows her head
as I bow mine!
2520   But I cannot hear the harmony
of her voice: now I will be quiet, and while
I am silent you will permit me, kind goddess,
to hear your dear, divine words.
Oh me! I am silent and she is silent, and if I
2525   appear to desire to speak with her,

she also appears to long for the same thing!
Alas, I feel already in my enflamed soul
a burning desire to possess
the celestial beauty that I look at in vain!
2530   O pure and clear spring,
who is this who dwells in your bosom,
by me never before seen? Who has taken me from myself
and robbed me of the dear liberty
to which I was accustomed,
2535   going around so haughty and merry? Wave, you were
born to cause my death!
      Wave, I do believe that your origin was
Phlegethon, since from your blow
I feel myself burst all into flames![22] Alas, I came
2540   to your coolness to appease the ardor
of my thirsty lips,
but a more ardent thirst
you have placed in the midst of my heart!
But you, who in the midst of the water ignite the fire,
2545   do not scorn my sincere faith
and my love, for to acquire them
a thousand weeping lovers pursued me.
Alas, my life, since nature does not allow me
to live with you in these waves,
2550   at least come dwell with me!
Join your hand with mine,
with which I will help you, and you then
will help me, my heart —
She extends her hand, oh, happy me!
2555   Yes, now, how content I am!
Come, come, my hope —
Oh, my vain thought!
I love a shadow! And in vain a shadow I desire!
O gentle slopes, hills, forests, woods, valleys —
2560   have you ever seen, ever heard that a nymph
encountered a sadder destiny than I?
Oh, hard, bitter luck!
I burst into flames and burn for myself, and alone

---

[22] See note 28 in the Introduction. The Phlegethon is a branch of the Styx, the river in Hades. The Phlegethon, as seen in its alternative name Pyriphlegethon, is a river of fire; thus, Ardelia relates her burning ardor to the flaming waves of this river.

I long to possess that which I possess the most!
2565   Oh, marvel! I would feel less pain
if the longed-for image
were more distant. Now how will I ever be able,
since I have my happiness with me,
to approach her mouth with mine?
2570   That which I most desire always comes with me,
I couldn't flee it, even if I wanted to!
Alas, how my peace
makes continuous war with me,
and this surpassing abundance
2575   makes me feel destitute of every pleasure!
Too much these eyes please my eyes,
this face, this breast, too much;
in the end, I love myself!
So, if I want to have revenge
2580   on the one who offends me, I must use cruelty
against myself; oh, unlucky love!
Eyes, true causes of my misfortune,
shed hot and bitter tears
justly to amend the unjust fire,
2585   because my heart only burned with your tinder!
Alas, alas! [I see] that for my great suffering,
while I cry over my misfortune, the weeping itself
is the cause of my distress —
because disturbing the water
2590   deprives me of the pleasure of myself!
I must, therefore, leave
to give this wave time to become as
tranquil as at first, so that I again
may enjoy gazing at myself!
2595   O spring, true spring of my misfortune,
if only I could leave with you all that fire
that (alas) I found in you!
Yet, in leaving I take with me
such a fire that [even] the wave where it was born
2600   can not extinguish it!
But I hope that since I have renewed
the cruel torture of wretched Narcissus,
like him destiny must put an end
to my pain with my death.

End of Act Four

ACT FIVE
SCENE ONE

Mirtilla, nymph, and Tirsi, shepherd

Mirtilla   You really must stop bothering me —
because I don't think about you at all!
Now calm down, for I'd rather abandon
this life of mine, if it still is mine,
than stop following my Uranio.

Tirsi   Perhaps you refuse to be my nymph,
believing that I live in
the forests or caves? But you deceive yourself
if you believe this! I am an inhabitant
of such a fertile and prosperous place,

2615   and so befriended by heaven that snow or ice
never assail it, and furious winds never
make war with it; only gentle and sweet
zephyr breezes blow there, giving life
to the plants and animals, to the grass

2620   always green and flowered; and the hills
always smell sweetly, and more sweet, the plain
smells of sage and mint
and of lilies, crocus, and violets.
There, you will always see the clever bee

2625   tasting the rich morning sweetness of
the lovely flowers.
There, each season the branches hang down,
loaded with fruit and adorned with beautiful flowers.
There, rivers and springs

2630   are of silver and pure crystal.
Neither among the flowers nor the grass

does a malevolent serpent hide,[1]
and neither aconite nor hemlock infects the fields and
    meadows
with deadly juice,
2635   nor do stinging nettles,
burdocks, thorn bushes, or other disagreeable plants
grow in the fertile and joyful fields.
There, beautiful Mirtilla, when the sun
burns its hottest, chatting with me
2640   or singing or lying in the bosom of the grass,
you may stay in the shade and weave a garland
of beautiful flowers for your golden hair.
Then, in the spring nearby
you may admire how beautiful you are!
2645   Meanwhile, I will carve your lovely name
and my heart gracefully bind with yours
in the tender bark
of many young trees.
Then I will say to them: "Grow,
2650   and may our loves grow with you!"
Then to the music of a reed pipe
I will sing of your beautiful face,
and I will make the stars resound
with your beauty and my good fortune!
2655   Alas, yield, Mirtilla!
Perhaps you do not understand this gift that I give you,
a cup of beechwood: there, in the bottom,
you will see carved a great mountain that appears to
support the stars, and above its high summit
2660   rests the moon
in the pose of a lascivious,
sylvan nymph
who, [having] abandoned her beautiful carriage,
sits with her charming Endymion.
2665   With her white hand
she shears the thick mantle from his little sheep,
then kisses her dear friend. Off to one side
Pan emerges from a nearby wood
and, revolted by her, he blazes up in anger,

---

[1] See Virgil, *Eclogue* 3.93 for a similar image of a snake in the grass.

2670   and he seems to unleash his tongue with these
              pronouncements:
       "How unworthy of the name of goddess you are,
       that a vile shepherd induces you, O damned one,
       to scorn a god so famous!
       Well I see now that you are
2675   as mutable of heart as you are of appearance,
       perfidious one, constant only in inconstancy!"
       You will see how art
       has molded these figures so well,
       so that not only sight has been tricked,
2680   but hearing has been deceived as well, because one seems
       to hear what one doesn't hear.
       I swear to you, my life, that for this [cup]
       Alcon once wanted to give me two calves,
       who had not yet felt the yoke!

Mirtilla   It will never be true
       that gifts can persuade me [to do]
       what reason denies,
       what a lover's passionate pleas might accomplish!
       It is with love that one buys true love
2690   and not with gifts! Therefore I thank you,
       and I beg you that for God's sake you will finally give up
       this vain and crazy enterprise of yours!
       And if you really want to please me, get out of here!

Tirsi   I will elect your will as
       most severe law for myself; I will depart,
       and I will give up this venture;
       but along with it, I will give up my life —
       You remain more cruel and fierce than beasts!

Mirtilla   [to herself] Could it be that he goes away
       prepared to do to himself that which he threatens?
       Unfortunately it will be only too true!
       And how will you endure
       being the cause of another's voluntary death,
2705   Mirtilla? Are you so cruel? Alas, look at
       what you are doing! But maybe he's faking —
       it may be, but I don't believe it:
       I don't know why I don't believe it, but I don't believe it,
       and I feel pity for him!

2710   Wretched one, I will follow him and, if possible,
            save him from a cruel death and myself from infamy!

                              SCENE TWO

                           Igilio, shepherd

Igilio   The vast sea can never have enough water,
            nor the piercing cicada dew,
            nor the humming bee thyme,
2715   nor the greedy kid cytisus,[2]
            nor is cruel Amor satisfied by tears!
            Cruel Amor, well do I see the sorry end
            you desire for my life,
            since beautiful Fillide, from whence comes my life,
2720   you make so indifferent to my weeping, and you render her
            so scornful and so deaf to these sorrowful words.[3]
            I will therefore by dying
            put an end to my misfortune, which has no end while I live!
            You, knife, who would so often
2725   write the name of her whom I adore,
            and would inscribe my pure faith for her
            in these green trees, whose growing
            increased my pain with my love,
            today in my breast you will be concealed!
2730   Therefore without fear, bold hand,
            wound where cruel Amore struck me:
            unleash this soul at last from the most sorrowful
            body that nature has ever formed!
            But before these eyes are closed in eternal sleep,
2735   I want with the same knife
            to leave written in this green tree
            the miserable ending of my life,
            so that from one tongue to another,
            from one ear to another,
2740   the news will spread of my cruel
            and pitiless Filli. Oh, why do I call her mine,
            since Amor doesn't want her to be mine?

---

    [2] Cytisus is commonly called broom.
    [3] Andreini writes, "... sì sorda a le dolenti note," which could also be translated, "so
deaf to these sorrowful *notes*," since these "words" might have been sung.

If throughout these woods
the story of my death lives on,
2745   let her hear it! I have no doubt
that death will entreat from her beautiful eyes
some kind little tear or some
hot sigh that was denied me in life.
Lucky death,
2750   since you alone will have
that which my living faith never could!

SCENE THREE

Filli, nymph, and Igilio, shepherd

Filli   [to herself] Now isn't that Igilio? It is he, himself — and
what will he do with that bare knife?
I will listen to him and observe him attentively
2755   to see what he's preparing to do.

Igilio   Air, sky, earth, and water,
and you, eternal lights
of day and of night,
be kind to this green tree,
2760   so that in its trunk eternally
these last words of mine remain engraved.
And you, sorrowful verses,
if any courteous wanderer longs
to know the hard end of my life,
2765   explain it to him thus:
HERE LIES THE FAITHFUL IGILIO,
who, loving Filli, had such a cruel fate,
that for her he hastened to a voluntary death.

Filli   [to herself] O words that could
2770   soften stones!

Igilio   Having fulfilled your first task,
my fearless right hand, you must now accomplish
the second extreme and
most cruel task
2775   in a dutiful and pitiless way!

Filli	Stop, Igilio, don't do it!
Igilio	Alas, who interrupts me?
Filli	It is I, don't you recognize me?
Igilio	Oh, cruel one, do you want me to live so that you may have me die a double death in life?

Filli   To give you not death, but a happy
life, just as you long for,
Amore has led me here!
I would certainly be a block of stone if,
having witnessed such solid proof from you,
2785   I didn't want to change my mind and my will! I give
     myself to you,
abandoning him who unworthily
held me for a time, bound fast by cruel ties.

Igilio   My eyes, what do you see?
My ears, what do you hear? Am I awake,
2790   or is this a dream?

Filli   If you don't believe your eyes and ears,
at least believe your hands that hold me
more tightly against you
than ivy embraces any tree!
2795   You are all my good fortune, Igilio, and
I, who am your Filli, have come
to satisfy you fully with my love.

Igilio   O day happier than any other
for me, O lucky day,
2800   since in one moment today I have acquired two lives!
My life (if I'm allowed to call you mine),
after so much toil and so much anguish
suffered for you, give me
a more strong and sure token
2805   of your new amorous flame.

Filli   Since even my soul,

which in the tip of my tongue[4]
came to speak with you,
cannot make you sure of my faithful faith,

2810   here I give you my hand
for a more secure pledge.

Igilio   O beautiful white hand,
how you withdraw me from the abyss and place me in heaven!
Now surely I hold you and sweetly I squeeze you —

2815   but come with me, my heart, for I want to announce
to my companions my happy destiny,
so much more precious, because so little hoped for!

Filli   We'll go wherever you want.

SCENE FOUR

Uranio, shepherd

Uranio   Amore, you make me flee the one who follows me,
2820   and follow the one who flees me!
Harsh law of Amore,
if being cruel is Amore's law.
But here is the one who with her beautiful eyes
has made of mine a fountain,

2825   and of my breast a burning forge.
I will lie in wait to hear
what she says, and if she yet regrets
treating me so cruelly.

SCENE FIVE

Ardelia, nymph, and Uranio, shepherd

Ardelia   [to herself] Still I am forced to return here where
2830   I lost myself, O cruel spring, O sole
cause of my sadness!

---

[4] Andreini writes, "Or poi che l'alma mia / che ne la sommità di questa lingua / venuta teco parla." Her soul has traveled all the way to her tongue to speak to him, but he doesn't believe her words.

Don't mind that by gazing
at your tranquil breast I take great pleasure in
admiring myself, and, if I disturbed
2835   your tranquillity with my weeping,
may the great desire that my heart feels
to enjoy myself be a sufficient excuse!

Uranio   [to himself] I know for sure that I do not deceive myself!
This is surely
the pitiless Ardelia who pines away for
2840   herself! O strange wonder —
O worthy punishment for proud beauty!
Oh, the incredible power of Amore!
I want to draw near her only to hear
if she has yet learned
2845   to show herself less cruel.

[to Ardelia] Now, proud and pitiless Ardelia,
at long last, you truly experience my pain
in your suffering,
as well as the powers of the great Amore!

Ardelia   I know him too well, and my failure I confess —
truly I can attest to everyone
his supreme power!
But if he would have me at the same time
become a lover and a beloved, he should have
2855   made me the lover of my lover
and not of myself! I can help others
little, and myself not at all,
since I love myself!

Uranio   This is worthy punishment
for your sin, but if you want to take pleasure in
2860   yourself, love your faithful Uranio!
For he is changed in you, my life,
through the power of Amore, so it follows
that by taking pleasure in me, you will take pleasure
in yourself;
thus, your labors
2865   and your love are not thrown to the wind!
And since you know your error,
make amends, if you don't want

heaven angry with you.
One may, when one wishes,
2870   unburden oneself of every sin, and whoever doesn't do it
brings upon himself [or herself] the highest
vengeance! Therefore take my advice:
Don't wait until your golden hair
becomes silver; your forehead,
2875   now so wide and pleasing,
wrinkles; your polished cheeks
where milk and blood mix
crinkle and fade; the ivory
enclosed in your mouth loses its whiteness,
2880   and the crimson roses of your lips
become (alas) pale violets!
Don't wait, Ardelia, until the horrible
infirmity of old age overtakes you!
Don't desire, my life, to squander
2885   the days and hours of your beauty,
for if you wait, [while] rapacious time
sets itself against you with all its strength,
you will repent of your mistake,
but you won't be able to remedy it,
2890   and, repentant, you will say:
"Why to the wise mind doesn't
strength return, and beauty to the body, and the years
flourishing and fresh? Why doesn't that age return to me,
when I could do so much, but see little?"
2895   But the words and your desires will be
lost in the air. It is nothing new
that repenting too late profits nothing,
and Jove laughs at vain and late
schemes: It is ill-fitting
2900   to be the servant of Amore in old age
as much as to be his enemy in youth!

Ardelia   Your wise counsel
is so powerful that I am ready
to change my will before I change my face!
2905   Now I free myself from falsehood, and I give myself to truth:
I desire to love a body and no more a shadow.
Uranio, I give and consecrate myself to you,
and I want to live and die yours!

Uranio	You certainly show just now that you are a woman,
2910	since you have persuaded yourself all of a sudden
	to make me wholly yours! Surely
	the beautiful feminine sex,
	among the many, many gifts
	that heaven and nature
2915	have granted it, also possesses counsel
	which is only the wiser for having been little pondered.
	Oh, my dear Ardelia, it is truly granted to me
	to have you for my spouse!
	I give you thanks, O sacred starry friends,
2920	O spring that in flowing issued forth
	with your waves my sweet salvation!
	I pray to heaven that, in recompense
	for my great happiness, you never
	become muddied. If this does not happen,
2925	since you were a minister and chief for Amore,
	I would pray to Jove that in the future
	the triform goddess will always wash
	her delicate, prized limbs in you;
	but perhaps the sun's sister would avoid
2930	bathing in you, for you
	have taken away the most beautiful nymph that followed her.
Ardelia	No, no, Cynthia doesn't despise anything
	that takes away her nymphs, though
	she holds them dear, as long as they are conducted
2935	to an honest and just end. She doesn't abhor Amore
	when to join them in marriage
	he inflames them for a happy and handsome shepherd;
	instead, she enjoys it, knowing
	that, if the nymphs were to be deprived
2940	of honest marital love, she would be
	deprived of servitude: and a kingdom is nothing
	without servants, as we are to her.
Uranio	I rejoice to hear such news,
	because if this beautiful spring
2945	will not have that good which I desire for it,
	at least it will not be spoiled by her hatred.
	And we, happy and secure, will enjoy
	life, happy and joyful!
	But come at last to my hut,

2950   or rather, your hut, where you will see written inside
         your beautiful name and my pain,
         and you will also see diverse things
         that I made for you when you scorned me
         and wanted to accept nothing from me: now I want
2955   you to take them with your beautiful hand and, also,
         with your frank finger, erase
         these gloomy words that once were
         a true sign of my grave sadness.
         Instead of these, you will write there
2960   these brief words:
         "Uranio was of all others the most unhappy,
         and now, through my mercy, he is the most happy."

Ardelia I will do what you desire; let's go at last!

Uranio   Let's go, my idol!

SCENE SIX

Tirsi, shepherd, and Mirtilli, nymph

Tirsi   Again I have met my sweet enemy,
         and, although I am armed with disdain,
         my ardent desire has not lessened;
         on the contrary, the more I see myself denied
         her beloved appearance, so much more I feel
2970   the stubborn desire grow in me!
         Nor through rebuffs is the knot loosened
         with which Amore binds and torments me!
         But how will I ever survive without the beautiful light
         from both her lights,[5]
2975   unless I try another life?
         Alas, deprived of her, I am deprived of myself,
         and thus Amore holds me,
         so that without end
         are my grave pains!
2980   Will I consequently suffer to sustain
         a life worse than death? Ah, it is not true!

---

[5] Andreini writes, "de l'una e l'altra luce," meaning "both her lights," but here it may also be translated as "both her eyes."

Flee, flee, my heart,
these cruel lights
with which Amore kills you,
2985   Amore who always searches out new spoils
to adorn his inflamed chariot!
Flee, afflicted eyes,
the killing air of that face which I
for my misfortune saw.
2990   Steps, that were scattered in following
the fleeing Mirtilla,
lead me, miserable and sorrowful,
upon the highest mountain
that there is here in Arcadia,
2995   so that, by hurling myself down from it,
[I will] put an end to my sorrow
with one sole torment;
although death is no torment
to a man afflicted, but rather
3000   an end to every torment! Therefore I go
to end my hard and bitter life,
since Amore and Mirtilla
long for my death.

Mirtilla   He who tries through death
3005   to flee the miseries
that the world carries with it
is full of every cowardice!
Don't you know that time, love, faith, and steadiness
never foil other people's hope?
3010   I heard, my Tirsi, all that
you said out of your great pain, how
distrust of Amore and Mirtilla
made you desire a worthless death
[by leaping from] this steep cliff. But if you really want
3015   to hurl yourself down, I want
my breast to be the precipice![6]

Tirsi   Had I discovered that my love
was, if not dear, at least
not disagreeable to you, then I could
3020   be called a vile coward,

---

[6] "Precipizio," or precipice, could also be translated as "ravine."

if I had decided to die
to avoid suffering this pain.
Yet, knowing beyond a doubt
that you followed Uranio,
3025   and having also heard it from your own tongue,
and having also recognized proof
that Amore had been angered by my ardor,
[those] were the reasons why I, despising life,
wanted to kill myself.
3030   But if I wanted to die
for your cruelty, it is also right
that for your pity I live and breathe!
So, I am truly happy and fortunate on earth
since my war⁷ here is finished.
3035   Courteous and godly Amore,
I give you thanks, for
you no longer want to torture me!
Oh, my beautiful Mirtilla,
you are truly content after all
3040   to accept my faith and to be mine!

Mirtilla   Tirsi, live certain
that I will never be another's,
but I am and will be yours as long as I live!

Tirsi   Oh, happy close bond of love,
3045   that so soon has indissolubly
tied together our better parts!
But who are these that we see coming toward us
so festive and full of joy? They are
Uranio, Ardelia, Igilio, and Filli, oh, beautiful couples;
3050   there is also Coridon, but where are they going?

SCENE SEVEN

Uranio, Tirsi, Igilio, and Coridone, shepherds.
Ardelia, Filli, and Mirtilla, nymphs.

Uranio   Heaven save you, Tirsi!

---

⁷ Andreini uses the word "guerra," which means "war," but may also be translated as "struggle." See commentary on Andreini's Petrarchism in the Introduction, xvi.

Tirsi   Welcome!
            Uranio, where are you going with such happy company?

Uranio   By common consent
            together we are going to the temple of Venus,
3055   for, by her mercy and that of her son,
            we are happy and content!
            And, because Amore doesn't long for
            any victim or sacrifice other
            than our hearts,
3060   allowing the other honors
            to his beautiful mother,
            to her we make devout sacrifice,
            and, in thanking her, we also thank
            her charming son.
3065   You are one of his new followers,
            if the truth about you resounds,
            [so] begin to adore him!

Tirsi   Certainly I want to do it, and wisely
            you reason that [by] honoring
3070   the son, one also honors
            the father, and thus
            [by] honoring the mother the son is honored!
            So, following your advice, I will
            give thanks to the goddess of the third heaven,[8]
3075   since by her mercy
            I live content and fortunate.
            Go on, Uranio, and we will then follow you!
            But here is Gorgo, who comes to us
            loaded with provisions; perhaps he
3080   will also want to praise Amore.

SCENE EIGHT

Gorgo, Uranio, Tirsi, Igilio, Coridone, shepherds.
Ardelia, Mirtilla, Fillide, nymphs.

Gorgo   Now you see, now you see
            why Damon will have been waiting for me:

---

[8] See Prologue, note 2.

I went to the hut, and I found
that Alfesibeo had just roasted
a good kid so fat
3085   that I was compelled to taste
only a hundred mouthfuls, and I drank
so reasonably that I fell asleep for quite a while,
and I believe that Damone
3090   may have died of hunger, the poor man!
I want to go find him —
Oh, what a beautiful troop of friends! Good-bye, shepherds,
good-bye, little nymphs!

Filli   Stop, you simpleton!

Gorgo   Why do you insult me, rude woman?
3095   As I touch my goats, they
are worth something.
But now I want to turn to these that seem
as tame as
my sheep: O big beautiful ones,
3100   let me touch you! Oh, what little hands,
soft as wool! I promise
that if I were among you,
you would run the risk of
making me fall in love,
3105   and if by chance you pleased me,
I would present to you
little kids as beautiful and wanton
as you are, sheep as white
as your hands, grapes as sweet
3110   as your lips,
calves just as soft and plump
as you are delicious!

Mirtilla   In the end, everything you say
comes down to eating!

Gorgo   And so, does it seem to you
that I don't govern myself wisely?

Mirtilla   Certainly,
if you govern yourself wisely
while following your taste.

Ardelia	Come on, Mirtilla, don't pay attention to that fellow any longer!
Gorgo	Because I am not handsome?
Uranio	Gorgo, turn around, listen to what I say!
Gorgo	Speak freely! I will listen to you.
Uranio	We, in common accord, want to give thanks to the divine goddess of love,
3125	so be quiet! And if it pleases you to honor this goddess with us, we will be greatly thankful to you, not to mention that you will fulfill your duty.[9]
Gorgo	Let's go! I am content — but you go ahead, so that I may follow
3130	and imitate you.
Uranio	Now then, listen, for I will begin as we have agreed, since we are at the temple of the goddess: These crimson roses, a clear and true sign
3135	of your amorous, burning desires, O beautiful goddess of Gnidus,[10] from their beloved nest I picked this morning, and reverently and humbly I consecrate to you. Now don't despise
3140	[this] trifling gift, but with a kind heart take it for my love.
Ardelia	This crown of beautiful flowers Ardelia humbly gives to you, mother of Amore and goddess of the third heaven,
3145	since with divine zeal

---

[9] The speeches on the gifts that follow this announcement are remiscent of dedicatory epigrams from Book VI of *The Greek Anthology*.

[10] Gnidus, or Cnidus, was a town where Venus, surnamed the Gnidian, or Cnidean, was the chief deity, and she had a temple there.

you have put an end to her fierce desires
by making her Uranio's beloved wife.

Igilio   This green myrtle[11]
            I happily consecrate to you,
3150   beautiful Venus, since for me all
            the martyrdoms, the tears,
            and the sighs are dead
            that were previously the fruits of my life:
            therefore, take it now
3155   as a testimony of my past woes.

Filli   This pure white dove[12]
            so dear to you (if the truth among us resounds)
            with pure and reverent affection
            I, too, consecrate to you.

Tirsi   Take this blood-red flower,
            that languishing dies
            and conceals the image of your beautiful Adonis,[13]
            among these leafy branches,
            O beautiful Cytheræa,[14]
3165   more beautiful than any other celestial goddess!

Mirtilla   This pure white
            veil, kind goddess,
            from whom always comes
            every joy and delight,
3170   I give to you as a sign of my faith
            so pure that it exceeds every whiteness.

Coridone   These beautiful little flowers
            that adorned a field
            my beautiful Nisa cut by hand
3175   at the break of day
            and in turn gave them to me:

---

[11] Myrtle was a sacred plant for Venus.

[12] The dove was one of Venus's favorite birds.

[13] At his death Adonis, Venus's beloved, was changed into an anemone (see Act Two, note 14).

[14] Andreini uses the name Citerea, or Cytheræa, which is a surname of Venus taken from Cythera, the island near which she sprang from the sea-foam.

reverently I consecrate them
to your beautiful image.[15]

Gorgo   Even though it is not my custom
3180   to make offerings to your divinity,
            nevertheless, I also happily desire,
            as I am wont to do,
            to give you something
            other than myrtle or a rose
3185   or other charming flowers,
            or a dove or a veil
            as these nymphs and shepherds have done
            for proof of their devoted zeal:
            Instead, behold, I will give you
3190   much better things to amuse you!
            The beloved fruits of Ceres and Bacchus
            I give you, for without these
            your dear treasures will be cold and frozen.[16]
            And behold how I will try them first
3195   so that you do not suspect perhaps
            that there was deadly poison [in them]!
            But first I will sit in the bosom of the grass.

Igilio   Yes, yes, feel free to sit down so that the wine
            goes easily to its place.[17]

Tirsi   Oh, how he gulps it! It appears exactly
            as if he swallows the vessel with the wine!

Gorgo   Now I seem to be better,
            though my palate
            has scarcely been sprinkled,
3205   but behold that again
            I return to fill the drinking-cup,
            and, as I promised, I freely give it to you!

---

[15] Andreini uses the word "simulacro," which means "image" or "statue."

[16] Another reference to the proverb from Terence's *Eunuchus*, line 732. See the discussion of this proverb in the Introduction, xiv.

[17] A play on Aristotelian physics: fluids flow downward. See Aristotle's *Physics*, Book 4.4: "Every place has the attribute of being up or down; and by nature each body travels to or remains in its *proper* place, and it does so in the direction of up or down." The translation is by Hippocrates G. Apostle.

But I must leave,
beautiful Venus: good-bye, shepherds, good-bye,
3210   nymphs, I leave you! Remain in peace
while I go to find my companion,
where on the fresh grass we will spread out
the common food
and there, with joy and feasting,
3215   we will eat together happily — good-bye, troop of friends!

Uranio   God likewise speed you! Igilio, Tirsi,
Coridone, Mirtilla, Ardelia, and Filli,
since we have partially fulfilled
our duties, and since Phœbus[18]
3220   inclines to the west,
it will be best to return to [our] paternal homes,
to celebrate among ourselves,
and every year on such a day,
as long as we live,
3325   I want us all together
to come to make sacrificial devotions
in this place, a faithful testimony
to our happy and fortunate loves.
We pray in the meantime that heaven
3230   smile always upon these agreeable fields,
that Zephyr breathe eternally
among these green leafy branches,
and that his beautiful Flora always spread flowers
throughout the valleys, hills, fields, and meadows.

Ardelia   May snow or freezing ice never hold back
the course of the swift rivers and springs,
and may never a flock with dirty feet
cloud their lucid waves,
so that their clear, tranquil streams
3240   always reflect the most beautiful nymphs.

Igilio   May wild beasts never be seen
on these friendly sloping hills,

---

[18] Phœbus refers to the sun.

but may the hearty farmer always see
Ceres's golden tresses waving.[19]

Filli   May Juno never disturb the tranquil air,
             or Jove ever with his irritated hand strike lightning
             among us, or his brother Neptune
             shake the mountain or the plain;
             may Nature always grant
3250   an eternal spring to this place.

Tirsi   May Apollo never deny his bright rays
             to this divine land,
             but may it be festive and pleasing,
             always full of flowers, always full of fruit.

Mirtilla   May these shores never be disturbed
             by the fury of Aquilo,[20]
             but may gentle breezes be perpetually in this place
             among the flowers, leafy branches, grasses, shadows, caves,
                 and waves.

Coridone   We go praising Amore
3260   and his beautiful mother,
             since by their mercy so many sorrows
             have had happy and fortunate ends.
             May fate always be favorable to this place,
             and may the nightingales in a contest
3265   among these green branches
             warble wanton little notes
             and with new desire
             sing always of love's highest delights!

The End

---

[19] Ceres was the goddess of agriculture, and she was especially associated with grains: hence, her "golden tresses" are the waving stalks of grain.

[20] Andreini uses "Aquilone," for Latin Aquilo, the big, strong North Wind.

BIBLIOGRAPHY

Alighieri, Dante. *The Inferno*. Trans. Charles Singleton. Bollingen Series 80. Princeton: Princeton University Press, 1970.

———. *Inferno*. Trans. Robert Pinsky. Milan: Arnoldo Mondadori, 1991. Repr. in *The Inferno of Dante*. New York: Farrar, Straus and Giroux, 1994.

Andreini, Isabella. *La Mirtilla*, ed. Maria Luisa Doglio, Serie rosa, 7. Lucca: Fazzi, 1995.

———. *La Mirtilla favola pastorale*. Verona: Francesco dalle Donne and Scipione Vargnano, 1599.

———. *Mirtilla pastorale*. 2nd ed. Verona: Sebastiano dalle Donne and Francesco Compagni, 1588.

———. *Mirtilla pastorale*. Milano: Bordoni and Locarni, 1605.

D'Aragona, Tullia. *Dialogo della infinità di amore*. In *Trattati d'amore del cinquecento*, ed. Giuseppe Zonta, 187–243. Bari: Laterza, 1912.

Aristotle. *Physics*. Trans. Hippocrates G. Apostle. Bloomington: Indiana University Press, 1969.

Baretti, Giuseppe Marco Antonio. *A New Dictionary of the Italian and English Languages*. Ed. John Davenport and Guglielmo Comelati. London: Simpkin, Marshall, and Company, c. 1854.

Bell, Robert E. *Women of Classical Mythology: A Biographical Dictionary*. Santa Barbara: ABC–CLIO, 1991.

Bordieu, Pierre. "The Forms of Capital." In *Handbook of Theory and Research for the Sociology of Education*. Ed. John G. Richardson, 243–58. New York: Greenwood Press, 1986.

Bulfinch, Thomas. *The Age of Fable*. New York: Airmont, 1965.

Clubb, Louise George. *Italian Drama in Shakespeare's Time*. New Haven: Yale University Press, 1989.

Daniel, Samuel. *The Queen's Arcadia*. In *Three Renaissance Pastorals*, ed. Elizabeth Story Donno, 183–250. Medieval & Renaissance Texts & Studies 102. Binghamton, NY: Medieval and Renaissance Texts and Studies, 1993.

Doglio, Maria Luisa. Introduction to *La Mirtilla*, by Isabella Andreini, 5–30.

Donno, Elizabeth Story. Preface and Introduction to *Three Renaissance Pastorals*, ix–xxxiii.

Erenstein, Robert L. "Isabella Andreini: A Lady of Virtue and High Renown." In *Essays on Drama and Theatre: Liber Amicorum Benjamin Hunningher*, 37–49. Amsterdam: Standaard, 1973.

Guarini, Battista. *Il pastor fido*. In *Three Renaissance Pastorals*, ed. Elizabeth Story Donno, 55–182.

The Greek Anthology. Trans. W. R. Paton. 5 vols. Vol. 1. The Loeb Classical Library. Cambridge, MA: Harvard University Press, 1960.

Hammond, N.G.L., and H. H. Scullard, eds. *The Oxford Classical Dictionary*. 2nd ed. Oxford: Clarendon, 1970.

Homer. *The Iliad*. Trans. Andrew Lang et al. Modern Library College Editions. New York: Modern Library–Random House, 1950.

——. *The Odyssey*. Trans. S. H. Butcher and A. Lang. Modern Library College Editions. New York: Modern Library–Random House, 1950.

Kerr, Rosalind. "The Actress as Androgyne in the *Commedia dell'Arte* Scenarios of Flaminio Scala." Ph.D. diss., University of Toronto, 1993.

Lea, K. M. *Italian Popular Comedy*. 2 vols. New York: Russell and Russell, 1962.

Lemprière, John. *Classical Dictionary*. London: Bracken, 1994.

MacNeil, Anne Elizabeth. "Music and the Life and Work of Isabella Andreini: Humanistic Attitudes Toward Music, Poetry, and Theater During the Late Sixteenth and Early Seventeenth Centuries." Ph.D. diss., University of Chicago, 1994.

Maylender, Michele. *Storia delle Accademie d'Italia*. 5 vols. Bologna: Licinio Cappelli, 1926–1930.

Ovid. "The Story of Phaeton." In *Metamorphoses*. Trans. Rolfe Humphries, 28–40. Bloomington, IN: Indiana University Press, 1983.

Peck, Harry Thurston, ed. *Harper's Dictionary of Classical Literature and Antiquities*. New York: Cooper Square, 1965.

Petrarca, Francesco. *The Canzoniere*. Trans. Mark Musa. Bloomington: Indiana University Press, 1996.

Pliny. *The Natural History of Pliny*. Trans. John Bostock and H. T. Riley. 6 vols. Vol. 3. London: Henry G. Bohn, 1855.

Raffel, Burton. *The Art of Translating Prose*. University Park: Pennsylvania State University Press, 1994.

Ray, Meredith Kennedy. "*La castità conquistata*: The Function of the Satyr in Pastoral Drama." *Romance Languages Annual* 9 (1998): 312–21.

Rebora, Piero, Francis M. Guercio, and Arthur L. Hayward. *Cassell's Italian Dictionary*. New York: Macmillan, 1967.

Richards, Kenneth, and Laura Richards. *The Commedia dell'Arte: A Documentary History*. Oxford: Basil Blackwell–Shakespeare Head Press, 1990.

Russell, Rinaldina, ed. *The Feminist Encyclopedia of Italian Literature*. Westport, CT: Greenwood Press, 1997.

Shakespeare, William. *A Midsummer Night's Dream*. In *The Riverside Shakespeare*, ed. G. Blakemore Evans et al., 217–49. Boston: Houghton Mifflin, 1974.

Smith, William, ed. *A Dictionary of Greek and Roman Biography and Mythology*. 3 vols. New York: AMS Press, 1967.

Speroni, Sperone. *Dialogo di amore*. In *Opere*, ed. Natale Dalle Laste and Marco Forcellini, 1–45. 5 vols. Venezia: Domenico Occhi, 1740; repr. with an introduction by Mario Pozzi, Rome: Vecchiarelli, 1989.

Stampino, Maria Galli. "Bodily Boundaries Represented: The Petrarchan, the Burlesque and Arcimboldo's Example." *Quaderni d'italianistica* 16 (1995): 61–79.

Stevenson, Jane. "Women and Classical Education in the Early Modern Period." In *Pedagogy and Power: Rhetorics of Classical Learning*. Ed. Yun Lee Too and Niall Livingstone, Ideas in Context 50. Cambridge: Cambridge University Press, 1998.

Stortoni, Laura Anna, and Mary Prentice Lillie, trans. *Women Poets of the Italian Renaissance*. New York: Italica, 1997.

Tasso, Torquato. *Aminta*, trans. Henry Reynolds. In *Three Renaissance Pastorals*, ed. Elizabeth Story Donno, 1–54.

Tassoni, Iacom'antonio. "Già di si nobil Donna. . . ." In *La Mirtilla Pastorale*, Milano: Bordoni e Locarni, 1605.

Taviani, Ferdinando. "Bella d'Asia: Torquato Tasso, gli attori e l'immortalità." *Paragone* 35 (1984): 3–76.

Terence. *The Eunuch* in *Terence*. Trans. John Sargeaunt, 232–351. 2 vols. Vol. 1. The Loeb Classical Library. Cambridge, MA: Harvard University Press, 1939.

Theocritus. *Thyrsis*. In *The Greek Bucolic Poets*. Trans. J. M. Edmonds, 9–23. The Loeb Classical Library. Cambridge, MA: Harvard University Press, 1960. Theophrastus. *Enquiry into Plants*. Trans. Sir Arthur Hort. 2 vols. Vol. 1. Cambridge, MA: Harvard University Press, 1961.

Virgil. *Eclogues*. In *The Idylls of Theocritus and the Eclogues of Virgil*. Trans. C. S. Calverley, 187–230. Bohn's Popular Library. London: G. Bell and Sons, 1913.

——. *Eclogues. Georgics. Aeneid I–VI*. Trans. H. Rushton Fairclough. Rev. G. P. Goold. Cambridge: Harvard University Press, 1999.

Zingarelli, Nicola. *Lo Zingarelli minore: vocabolario della lingua Italiana*. 12th ed. Bologna: Zanichelli, 1994.